Anonymous

African Servitude : When, Why, and by Whom Instituted

By Whom, and how long, shall it be Maintained?

Anonymous

African Servitude : When, Why, and by Whom Instituted
By Whom, and how long, shall it be Maintained?

ISBN/EAN: 9783337249199

Printed in Europe, USA, Canada, Australia, Japan

Cover: Foto ©ninafisch / pixelio.de

More available books at **www.hansebooks.com**

AFRICAN SERVITUDE:

WHEN, WHY, AND BY WHOM

INSTITUTED.

BY WHOM, AND HOW LONG,

SHALL IT BE

MAINTAINED?

READ AND CONSIDER.

I remember the days of old; I meditate on all thy works.—*Ps.* cxliii. 5.

𝔑𝔢𝔴 𝔜𝔬𝔯𝔨:

DAVIES & KENT, STEREOTYPERS,

118 NASSAU STREET.

1860.

AFRICAN SERVITUDE.

God, the Almighty, the Creator of the Heavens and the Earth, and the Righteous Governor of the Universe, *did*, in the beginning of the world, when He had prepared it for man's abode, make man in his own spiritual image; gave him full dominion of the earth, supplied his wants, and granted unto him free intercourse or communion with Him, his Creator and Benefactor; requiring of man obedience to his expressed commands.

Adam, the first man, deliberately broke the first command, by which act, and the spirit of disobedience he allowed in his heart, he fell from his high estate, hid, and cut himself off from communion with his God, and made both his body and soul subject to death.

This grievous offense of Adam against his Maker, God, the only source of light, life, and happiness in the universe, must of itself, according to the eternal laws of Truth and Order (whether God expressly said so or not), separate him from his Friend and Creator, causing the deliberate offender (unless reconciled) ever to recede from God, into the dark sea of misery and death.

The loss or death of all that was good and happy, and the knowledge or gain of all that was evil and miserable (the marks of which we all bear), are the results of the first offense.

Woman, the partner God had given to man, being the leader in the first great transgression, advises her husband to take part with her in it, and through *her* means he is deceived, and it seems in consequence thereof she fell from her state of equality with man— lost her equal right to counsel, judge, execute, and govern in the affairs of the world, and was worthily made subject to man or to her husband.

But this loss to woman is for time only, not for eternity, for the Redeemer of man finally restores all things to those who belong to Him.

God, in his goodness, adapted woman to her true position; gave her a will and heart to obey, and made the relation of husband and wife, in its true life or sense, desirable, happy, and blessed.

But woman's subjection to her husband hindereth not her happiness for time, or salvation for eternity; in fact, they are both promoted and secured in the exercise by her of a true spirit of obedience and submission to her condition and calling, and also by the discharge of the duties belonging to her, having faith in the appointed Saviour.

The family was instituted by God. In all its relations and results it is the most important, the happiest, and the most blessed institution with which He has endowed the human race.

He has placed great power and corresponding honor and responsibility on the united head of the family. For its use and influence God holds its head in a measure accountable to Him. The head of the family should teach its members to fear, love, and obey the Creator, who has the right, and ought to be, the God of every family. He has threatened to pour out His fury upon all the families that will not call upon His name.

The power or government that God has given to parents for a time, over the members of the family, is the most arbitrary known in the world; a government that the most powerful emperors and kings care not to intermeddle with.

The families of the old world became wicked and corrupt, it would seem, because the sons of God, or godly men, rejected the counsels of their fathers, and allied themselves with the wicked families of the earth, so that soon all were estranged from God. "Wickedness and violence filled the earth;" God determined, in his righteous judgment, to destroy the race. Noah, an honored patriarch, or ruler of a family, the ninth in descent from Adam, described as "a just man, perfect in his generations, walking with God," in the midst of the wicked and corrupt inhabitants of the earth, did find favor in the eyes, not of men, but of the Lord, and was informed of the flood of waters that God should "bring upon the earth, to destroy all flesh wherein is the breath of life from under heaven." Noah was instructed by Him to prepare an ark for the deliverance of himself and family when the deluge should come. He believed and obeyed the Lord, and with his wife and his three sons, with their wives, were preserved from the flood. These eight persons were monuments of God's saving mercy, and witnesses of His great power and righteous judgments.

The Patriarch Noah, being 600 years old, was now the head and father of the human family, the great representative of the race. He was the object of God's favor, and received from Him special and general directions for the government of the world.

So far as we can learn from the Bible, there was no human power or governor set up over the people higher than the patriarchal head or father of the family.

The Patriarchs were Rulers and Priests as well as Fathers. God is the author of all fatherhood, therefore children, or members of the family, must render to the head of it such obedience as the Lord requires.

The family government is truly the foundation of all other government, and it may yet, in the future, become the governing influence of the world. It may, in some respects, be a type of that one whole family in heaven and earth, mentioned by St. Paul in his Epistle to the Ephesians.

God is our Father in Heaven, and our Saviour teaches us to call Him so when we come to Him in prayer.

Noah became a husbandman, planted a vineyard, and, partaking too freely of the fruit of the vine, exposed himself to shame. The Scriptures do not state that he was guilty of anything more than an act of imprudence. In his exposed state he was discovered by his younger son, probably his grandson Canaan, who informed his father Ham, and one or both of them, so far from feeling or expressing grief for the dishonor of their parent, exultingly informed others of it, glorying in his shame, despising his power and authority, and his office as ruler and priest of God to them and the rest of their father's family, lightly esteeming also his parental blessing, as well as the blessing of God.*

A true spirit of filial regard, love, honor, and obedience moved Shem and Japheth to protect their father; just the reverse of that which influenced their brother Ham to dishonor him. On the part of the former, it was an act of faith; of the latter, unbelief. The sin of Ham was not only great, but aggravated. He was probably more than six-score years old; for Canaan, his fourth son, all born after the flood, must have been old enough to discern between right and wrong, to have received the curse that fell upon him. Ham had seen the wickedness of the inhabitants of the old world, and knew they were destroyed because of their sins, which ought to have been a sufficient warning to him, not only to walk in the way of righteousness, but to command his family, and bring them up in the fear of the Lord, which it seems he did not do. He knew that

* Ham, who espied his father in this condition, instead of concealing his weakness, proclaimed it aloud, and to his other two brothers, Shem and Japheth, made him the subject of his scorn and derision. But, so far were they from being pleased with his behavior in this respect, that, taking a garment and laying it upon both their shoulders, they went backward till, coming to their father, they dropped the garment upon him, and so covered the nakedness which their pious modesty would not permit them to behold.—STACKHOUSE's *History of the Bible*.

God had chosen his father as the honored head of the human family, declaring him faithful, and communicating to him his designs. It was with Noah and his sons, including Ham, that God, after the flood, made or renewed with them his covenant, giving them and their posterity his promised blessing. In refusing to honor his parent, he refused to honor all governors, natural, civil, ecclesiastical, human, and divine. The sin was a representative one, and, under the circumstances, it was no light one in Ham and his son. It manifested in them no love for their parent, but an evil heart of unbelief toward God. For this offense the verdict of men and angels would at least be—that the disobedient should forfeit their rights, and privileges, and be brought into subjection to the obedient. What the judgment of the Almighty was, we have recorded in his sure Word—Genesis ix. 24–28; and although the record is very brief, yet it is clear and plain to the candid mind. It states that Noah, after a full knowledge of all that had transpired—what his younger son had done unto him—said, "Cursed be Canaan; a servant of servants shall he be unto his brethren. And he said, Blessed be the Lord God of Shem, and Canaan shall be his servant. God shall enlarge Japheth, and he shall dwell in the tents of Shem, and Canaan shall be his servant."*

In this instance, as in others, the curses as well as the blessings of the patriarchs are prophetical in their nature—to be fulfilled in future ages. This deliberate denunciation of Noah proceeded not from a spirit of indignation, but of prophecy. He was moved by the spirit of God to utter what he did—"For the prophecy came not in old time by the will of man, but holy men of God spake as they were moved by the Holy Ghost." As a prophet of the Lord, he foretold the consequences of the acts of his sons in this matter. The judgments that should follow the one, the blessings that should rest upon the others, as God, in His righteous will and pleasure, had seen fit to dispense, and which in time He would surely execute and fulfil.

It must be evident to every candid mind, that in this brief

---

* Bishop Lowth thus translates these important verses:

   "Cursed be Canaan;
   A servant of servants to his brothers let him be.
   Blessed be Jehovah, the God of Shem,
   And let Canaan be their servant.
   May God extend Japheth,
   And may he dwell in the tents of Shem,
   And let Canaan be their servant."

Ham signifies heat, burnt, or black; Japheth, persuasion, enlargement; Canaan, extreme humiliation.—Bush.

prophetic annunciation of what should follow his posterity, that a condition of servitude is laid upon the children of Ham, especially upon Canaan; and that the posterity of Shem and Japheth should have the benefit of their service.

God, who knows the end from the beginning, and is acquainted with the hearts of all men, for wise purposes allowed the faith of the three sons of Noah to be tried, and Ham was found wanting. In consequence of his lack of faith, his sinful conduct or defection, and that of his family, the Judge of all the earth deprives him and his children from their equal position in the great human family, and in His righteous judgment determines that they shall be made subject to, or become servants to, the rest of the families of the earth. From that time forth, actual servitude of some sort became their *normal condition*—was, and is, the *judicial* law of their race. Our first parents broke the first command on the first table, by disobeying the true God, and obeying that usurper, the devil, the god of the world—the legal consequence of which was death of body and soul. Ham, the son of Noah, broke the first command on the second table, by scorning and deriding his father, the legal consequences of which seems to be death of his body, or the forfeiture of it for the benefit of others.

God's moral laws are ever the same, promulgated or not. The law of God, as given by Moses, states in Exodus xxi. 15th and 17th verses : "He that smiteth his father, or his mother, shall surely be put to death." "He that curseth his father, or his mother, shall surely be put to death."

James Fisher, the Scotch divine, in his comment, says : "This severe punishment was inflicted for these crimes because either beating or cursing of parents are sins directly opposite to the light and law of nature, and frequent evidences, not only of the worst kind of ingratitude, but of incurable disobedience; and, therefore, the equity of this punishment seems to be approved by our Lord, under the New Testament—Matt. xv. 4."

If the parent was guilty of neglect of duty, the guilt of the child would be less. It can not be said that Noah was guilty of neglect, for he was declared faithful in all his generations.

From the Word of God, there can be no doubt that for a time a condition of servitude was inflicted upon the descendants of Ham, in whole or in part—in all probability the whole. It may be said of Ham, that in Canaan his seed should be called. Poole, in his Annotations, states, that "Interpreters have invented several other reasons why the curse, which properly belonged to Ham, was inflicted on his son Canaan—as, 1st. When Canaan is mentioned,

Ham is not exempted from the malediction, but rather more deeply plunged into it, because parents are apt to be more affected with their children's misfortunes than their own, especially if they themselves brought the evil upon them by their own fault or folly. 2d. God having blessed the three sons of Noah at their going out of the ark, it was not proper that Noah's curse should interfere with the Divine blessing, but very proper that it should be transferred to Canaan, in regard to the future extirpation of the people which were to descend from him. But—3d. Some imagine that there is here an ellipsis, or defect of the word father, since such relative words are frequently omitted, or understood, in Scripture. Thus, Matt. iv. 21: James of Zebedee, for *the son* of Zebedee. Acts vii. 16: Emmor of Sychem, for *the father* of Sychem, which our translation rightly supplies; and in like manner Canaan may be put for the father of Canaan, as the Arabic translation has it, *i. e.,* Ham, as the Septuagint here renders it. And though Ham had more sons, yet he may here be described by his relation to Canaan, because in him the curse was more fixed and dreadful, reaching to his utter extirpation, while the rest of Ham's posterity in after-ages were blessed with the saving knowledge of the Gospel."

That there might not in after-ages be any mistake or doubt upon whom the curse was laid, it would seem that the Almighty put upon the descendants of Ham, not only the black mark of disobedience and condemnation to service, but also prepared and adapted both mind and body for the service required of them.

The fall, or defection of Ham, considered in all its results, is one of the most, if not the most, important event to the human race that has transpired since the flood; save, always, the advent and death of the Saviour, the great event of the universe.

Before this important event (the fall of Ham) it might be truly said that " all men were born free and equal" in rights and privileges, but after this curse, who shall say, in opposition to God's Word, that there is an equality in conditions, rights, and privileges of all the inhabitants of the earth?

To assert that *all* men are born free and equal in rights, privileges, and conditions, is to say what every man of common sense knows to be untrue. To assert that *all* men ought to be, is to call in question the wisdom and goodness of God. To say that *all* men will be, is to declare that which has not yet been revealed.

Let us take the history of the world as we find it recorded in the Bible and other approved books; and we shall find that this condition or dispensation of servitude resting upon the children of

Ham, as far back as we have any authentic history of the race after the flood.

Those old patriarchs, Abraham, Isaac, and Jacob, had their servants, or bond men and women, in great numbers. A system of servitude had already, at that time, become a known and established condition in society.

We find, in times past, the prophetic declarations of the Patriarch Noah have been fulfilled, and that the curse and the blessing extend to our day, and are still in process of fulfillment according to God's sure Word.

The venerable Dr. Mede says : "There never has been a son of Ham who has shaken a scepter over the head of Japheth. Shem has subdued Japheth, and Japheth has subdued Shem, but Ham never subdued either."

That inspired servant of God and prototype of our Saviour, by the command of God, gave to the children of Israel the following permission, direction, and command, as found in Leviticus xxv. 44-46 : "Both thy bondmen, and thy bondmaids, which thou shalt have, shall be of the heathen that are round about you; of them shall ye buy bondmen and bondmaids. Moreover, of the children of the strangers that do sojourn among you, of them shall ye buy, and of their families that are with you, which they begat in your land : and they shall be your possession. And ye shall take them as an inheritance for your children after you, to inherit them for a possession ; they shall be your bondmen forever : but over your brethren the children of Israel, ye shall not rule one over another with rigor."*

Here the Israelites have full permission from the Almighty to buy, hold, and use forever the services of the heathen, or Canaanites, about them, who were descendants of Ham. Yet, we do not consider these texts, or this permission, as the foundation for their right to hold these heathen as bond men and women forever. We consider this portion of Scripture as containing a new writ, or warrant of execution, for the services of the Canaanites, issued to Moses and the children of Israel by the great Judge of the earth, upon the old judgment rendered in the days of Noah, 850 years before.

Besides the directions given, these texts are valuable to us, because they show that God remembers His word, and will both perform it and accomplish His designs. The posterity of Shem are reminded of their right to the services of the descendants of Canaan. We, the children of Japheth, have also a right to the services of the descendants of Canaan, or Ham, according to that

* Marginal reading—"Serve yourselves of them."

old, yet still living and abiding, dispensation of the Most High to the sons of Noah.

Shem and Japheth are not to blame for this condition of servitude abiding upon Ham; and if there is any advantage in receiving his service—as it seems there must be, for it is pronounced by Noah as a blessing—they have, for the honor and obedience they rendered to their parent, a right to it given them by the Almighty.

For reasons given in the preceding pages, we use promiscuously, as meaning or included in the same, the phrase, posterity of Ham, or descendants of Canaan. That the black race, or tribes of men inhabiting Africa, are the descendants of Ham, there can be no reasonable doubt, and it is not necessary to prove it here; in speaking of them, or the Africans, we shall consider that they are of the posterity of Ham, upon whom God has put his indelible mark, or *prima facie* evidence, to all that they belong not to the posterity of Shem or Japheth.

We use the terms service, servitude, and servants, instead of slavery or slaves, as being more Scriptural, and conveying a true import or meaning of the prophetical curse and blessing under investigation. As to slavery, there is no slavery like sin; the devil only truly owns slaves, and if we are free from him, we are free indeed.

That verse—Gen. ix. 37—containing the important and comprehensive prediction concerning Japheth and Shem and Canaan, is rendered different from King James' version by some translators. One old translation, published about the year 1600 (before King James' version), renders the verse thus: "God *persuade* Japheth, that he may dwell in the tents of Shem, and let Canaan be his servant;" and the following is the marginal note of comment: "Or enlarge or cause to return." "He declareth that the Gentiles which came of Japheth, and were separated from the Church, should be joined to the same by the persuasion of God's spirit, and preaching of the Gospel." The above seems to convey, as far as it goes, a true purport or correct meaning of this most important prediction, and comprehensive one, as regards the period of time covered and the people involved. Bear in mind, that a blessing is pronounced on Shem and Japheth. It could be no blessing to Shem to have Japheth dwell in his tents, or hold and occupy his temporal possession. It seems more consistent with the whole passage to adopt the spiritual meaning, that Japheth shall, through the influence of God's spirit, receive and enjoy all the privileges and blessings of the Gospel, given first to Shem, though now lost or discarded by him. According to St. Paul—Rom. xi. 25—it shall be enjoyed by both when the fullness of the Gentiles be come in. The reasons and evidence that can be given in favor of this interpretation of the prophecy outweigh all others. This brings the fulfillment of the prophecy down to and through the Gospel ages. And there is no escaping the conclusion, that in the Gospel ages, or in the times when Japheth shall possess and enjoy the Gospel, then he shall also have *Canaan* to be *his servant.* What reasons can be given, or proof brought to show, that we ought to limit this prophecy—the blessing and the curse—to the days of the Israelites and Canaanites of old? We have as, as yet, seen none.

The interpretation advocated here of the true meaning of Gen. ix. 37 is supported by the events of time, by the workings of God's providences, which truly explain His predictions and unfold His designs:

> " God's purposes will ripen fast,
> Unfolding every hour ;
> The bud may have a bitter taste,
> But sweet will be the flower.
> Blind unbelief is sure to err,
> And scan His work in vain—·
> God is His own interpreter,
> And He will make it plain."—COWPER.

In His Word it is written: "*He hath done whatsoever He pleased,* and *He giveth not account of any of His matters* " It does not become Him to stoop and explain His designs to carping mortals. His works of providence in time, and through eternity, do, and will, develop and explain all His plans, to His praise and the admiration of His creatures.

African servitude we hold, then, is not from man, but from God, dispensed in His wisdom and judgment to the posterity of Ham in consequence of sin. If it was a system of wrong and oppression, devised and maintained by the selfish will and power of men alone, it would not have stood a century, instead of reaching back over forty centuries, or more than one hundred generations. If the institution had its origin alone in the design or will of man, the righteous Governor of the world would have long since moved the so-called oppressed to have asserted their rights, achieved their freedom, and punished their adversaries.

We have no other resource, then, but to turn the whole matter over to the Almighty. Of ourselves we are not able to hold or maintain the system, but He is all-sufficient. Whatever good there is in the institution, ascribe to Him—the evil, take to ourselves.

If the system of servitude imposed upon the posterity of Ham is based upon God's *purpose,* as we believe it is, man can not overthrow

it; and those who see good in it need not fear. There is no sufficient reason to believe God will release the posterity of Ham from
the condition imposed until He has removed the mark of servitude
He has put upon them.

As the preservation of the Jews as a separate people, though min-
gled for ages among all the nations of the earth, is considered a
standing miracle, so we believe that this institution of bond-servants—this system of African servitude—will yet be considered a
standing evidence of God's sovereign will and power, of His wisdom
and goodness, and of the truth of His sure word and prophecy, of
which our Saviour said that "He came not to destroy, but to
fulfill;" and "till heaven and earth pass, one jot or tittle shall in no
wise pass from the law till all be fulfilled."

Who shall complain because the Almighty, in His sovereign will
and righteous judgment, saw fit for cause to lay upon a part of the
human family a condition of servitude to the rest? "Will not the
Judge of all the earth do right?" Let us not teach any who are
under the cloud to complain of any of the dispensations of God,
and say, "Why hast Thou made me thus?" "As the potter has
power over the clay to make of the same lump one vessel unto
honor and another unto dishonor, so God can and will do with His
creatures as He pleases, and none shall ever be able to charge Him
with unrighteousness." God has the same right to condemn one
portion of the race to servitude for a particular sin in the father,
that He had in condemning the whole race to death for disobedience
in the first parents of all. Who will have the hardihood to set his
wisdom against that of the all-wise God, and say it is not good for
the bodies or souls of men, for time or eternity, that men should be
adjudged to labor, and earn their bread by the sweat of their
brows? Who will put his kindness and consideration against the
goodness and mercy of God, and say that it was not kind to *woman*
that the Great Disposer of all should make her subject to her husband, and that her happiness and usefulness in this life were to be
found in true and constant efforts to perform the duties of the station assigned her? And who shall say it is neither wise nor good
for the African race (the descendants of Ham) to be in the service
of other portions of the human family, and that the relation of master and servant is not alike necessary and beneficial to both? God
can fit us for the station in life He intends we shall occupy, and give
us such measure of intellect, strength of body, and power of endurance, that we shall be perfectly adapted to our condition or calling,
and unfitted for any other. "As your day is, so shall your strength
be." It is our duty with faith and patience to perform the duties

of our condition or station in life, for therein lies our happiness and salvation.

When the earth was cursed for man's sake, we do not understand that any moral curse was put or charged upon it, but that it was in a measure deprived of those healthful or productive influences that should make it bear in abundance of all that was good, and only that which was good, for the living beings upon it.

So, when the posterity of Ham are cursed, we do not understand that a moral curse is pronounced upon and still hanging over them, but that they are made to stand lower in their position in the human family, and are deprived of their equality among their brethren of rights and privileges that they all before enjoyed in common; that there is nothing in the curse *per se* that prevents salvation, that hinders their coming to God through Jesus Christ. This state, or certain degree of servitude (now their normal condition), is not itself a barrier or preventive to their reception of the Gospel; and more than that, we hold to be true the doctrine, that submission to and rendering of the bond-service imposed upon the Africans (the posterity of Ham) actually tends to promote their well-being in this life and their eternal salvation.

We may believe that He who declared a soul to be of more value than the whole material world, would see to it that none of His dispensations to the human family should of themselves prove a hindrance to their salvation.

The righteous Governor of the world did and has sold his people Israel for short periods of time, and for generations, into the hands of wicked nations, because they turned away from, forgot, and disobeyed their Benefactor. Has He not the same right to dispose of the services of the degenerate children of a rebellious son to their more righteous brethren? If God in His wisdom sees fit to do this, as His Word declares He has done it, has, He not both the power and grace to adapt these degenerate children to the condition He has prepared for them? and can He not also, by His spirit, dispose those who receive these services of others, that they shall so deal with those, their servants, or bond men and women, that God's wisdom and mercy shall be praised, lives benefited, and souls saved? If it is better for woman, in view of time and eternity, to continue in the particular sphere marked out for her by God, rather than seek to fill some unnatural position not designed for her, why may it not be best for the African to occupy and perform (for time only) the duties belonging to a second-rate position in the human family, evidently assigned him by the Sovereign Disposer of all?

As the law of God (so just, yet so hard for us to obey) is a schoolmaster, to bring us to Christ the Saviour, so may not the condition of servitude be found necessary to bring those upon whom it is laid to the light, freedom, and salvation of the Gospel?

Do the facts concerning African servitude in this, our Gospel land, prove or lead us to believe that that condition tends to promote, more than any other, their temporal good and eternal happiness? We feel assured that they do. The fact that more than half a million of the colored population of the South are enrolled as members of the Evangelical churches, besides thousands who are not members, but seem to have and to exercise the faith of a true Christian, is an evident proof that there is a blessing somewhere for them in this institution, or dispensation, and that fruit thereof somehow grows from it unto eternal life.

On investigation it will be found, we believe, that a much larger proportion of the colored population of the South profess the Christian faith than in the free States at the North. And further, from all the information we have been able to gather, there is not much doubt but that the proportion of the colored population at the North at this time actually receiving and obeying the truths of the Gospel, is less than at the time when slavery was abolished in all the now free States of the Old Thirteen. At and before that time our New England fathers felt interested, and in a measure responsible for, the moral as well as physical well-being of their own servants, and taught them (as was the custom of many) the truths of the Gospel, and the doctrines as contained in their catechisms; they also, by proper restraint as well as example, caused their servants to obey, in a goodly measure, the precepts of the Bible.

From what we have personally seen at the South, we rejoice to know that multitudes of the Africans receive in simple faith the saving truths of the Gospel, and live contented and happy in the peaceful enjoyments of its hopes.

For example, take the city of Charleston, in South Carolina—(a State where the regulations concerning slavery, or bond-servants, are the most stringent, as are generally admitted)—in that city we have seen, in the morning, afternoon, and evening of the Sabbath days, summer and winter, the large galleries of the churches belonging to the Methodist, Baptist, Presbyterian, and Episcopal denominations, particularly the former, filled to overflowing with the colored population of that city, drinking in with joy the water of life that flows from those wells of salvation. They hear, seem fully to understand, believe, receive, and rejoice in the Gospel, which is as faithfully preached in the churches of that city, and at the South, as it is at the North. In that city we have been deeply impressed with the truth and preciousness of that blessing pronounced by the Redeemer, when He said, " Blessed be ye poor, for yours is the kingdom of God."

In no part of our country are the laboring population better provided and cared for than the African race at the South. If we believed that the system of African servitude, in its best and true sense, *hindered* the salvation of their souls, we could not defend it. But we believe the reverse—that the burden that is laid upon them is meant and works for their good.

Those acquainted with the African character know that they do not possess that power of reason, soundness of judgment, strength of resolution ; that perseverance, and nerved and fixed purpose of mind, stability of character, and power to resist evil influences and temptations, that are possessed by the whites ; but that in faith and love, in honest simplicity, frank expression of feelings, they are equal to the other races ; and that in contentment, docility, meekness, patience, and power of endurance, they excel the whites.

These prominent and important traits of character fit them for the important place, and that only, though a subordinate one, that God intended they should occupy, as we learn from his Word and providence. From their service the whites receive (and that with a good conscience) a certain measure of comfort and prosperity. The posterity of Ham, in living among the whites and rendering service to them (especially in our country), have an enhanced degree of health, length of life, comfort, security, quietness, freedom from care, and a participation in the blessings of the Gospel, as dispensed in our land. They have, also (singular though it may seem, yet generally a fact), a degree of pride and satisfaction in the prosperity of their masters, enhanced as it has been by their services— a sort of consciousness "that they have done what they could." "The sleep of the laboring man is sweet, whether he eat little or much," said the wise man. (He who made all things well, made it so that the laboring man should take his portion and rejoice in his labor.)

It is asserted that the system of slavery, or African servitude, in any degree is cruel and unjust. Those who are best acquainted with the system in our Southern States do not believe it, and know that it is not necessarily so, and that there are no evils connected with it but that might all be remedied.

It is charged that the masters of the Africans are naturally inclined to ill-treat and oppress them. The rule is just the reverse. It is proverbial that the white overseer at the South is more kind and compassionate than the black overseer. The white man is more lenient, and endures with patience the stupidity, obstinacy, and laziness of the black servant more than he does any other class. The renowned and learned Calmet wrote near one hundred and fifty years ago, that " 'Tis a tradition among the Eastern writers, that Noah, having cursed Ham and Canaan, the effect of his curse was, that not only their posterity were made subject to their brethren and born, as we may say, in slavery, but that likewise all on a sudden the color of their skin became black (for these Eastern writers maintain that all the blacks descended from Ham and Canaan); that Noah, seeing so surprising a change, was deeply affected with it, and begged of God that He would be pleased to inspire Canaan masters with a tender and compassionate love for him, and that his prayer was heard. For notwithstanding we may still at this day observe the effect of Noah's curse in the servitude of Ham's posterity, yet we may remark likewise the effect of his prayer, in that this sort of black slave is sought for and made much of in most places."—CALMET's *Dictionary, on the word Ham.*

The fact that Noah thus prayed rests, as some will maintain, upon tradition only. Admit it. We know that as a father he would pity his children; that as a good and righteous man he would intercede and pray for them, and that the prayer-hearing God would hear, and, as far as He thought best, *alleviate* the curse, and bring good out of it.

It is, in fact, owing to this natural feeling of compassion for the blacks, possessed in a measure by the whites (implanted within them by their Maker), that we have such a disposition to sympathize with them in their state of servitude, so that we allow our natural feelings of kindness to go too far or take a wrong direction, seeking present deliverance for the body only, by abolishing or nullying this condition of servitude, when God's providence and our practical experience do not favor it, nor his Word require it, nor the happiness and welfare of the blacks demand it.

In the practical exercise of the principles of true benevolence—of love and charity—it is not certain that it is the will of God that we should put forth effort to change the calling of any class of men; but the opposite seems to be true. It is our duty and privilege to do good, as we have opportunity, to all classes of men in their present calling or condition. If we bend all our efforts to change the calling of men, and not to improve them in their present condition, we at least seemingly work against God's providence, worse than waste our energies, and bring about a disturbed and injurious state of affairs. It is better, as the inspired St. Paul wrote, " That every man abide in the same calling wherein he was called." " For he that is called in the Lord, being a servant, is the Lord's freeman ; likewise also he that is called, being free, is Christ's servant. Let every man wherein he is called therein abide."

Would it not be the part of wisdom in all those who are labor'ng to change the calling or relieve the African race from the condition of servitude resting upon them, to hesitate and stop, until they find and produce from God's Word undoubted support and authority for their acts.

A careful examination of the past history of the white and black races, and of the opinions and acts of the mass of the people of the present day, make it evident to all who are willing to draw legitimate conclusions on the subject, that the two races can not live quietly and harmoniously together in a state of EQUALITY. For peace' sake, the black must give place to the white, or in some way come under a ondition of servitude to him. Even now the legislatures of many of our States are pressed by the people to pass laws expelling the free blacks, or preventing their settlement within the bounds of the State.

But there is no difficulty or disturbance in those communities where the blacks take their true position, and are in a certain degree in subjection to the whites. From the history of the African race there is abundant proof that they thrive not well alone, separated from the white races. Alone they make no progress in civilization, arts, and commerce. They can not maintain, and so can not reap, the benefits of free constitutional governments. They are enslaved and bound down to vice, crime, and misery. The Africans seem not able to stand alone among the nations, or to live intermingled among other nations, only as they are in some degree subservient to them.

As the vine twines about the oak for support, so the black loves to dwell near the white, and enjoy the security and support there is in his presence. When he is in his proper place, there is a mutual and reciprocal feeling of love and dependence that tends to promote the comfort and happiness of both. " The strong ought to bear the weak."

It certainly seems that God intended the races should dwell together in the relations He appears to have ordained.

Many have wondered why the colored population refuse to immigrate, and establish free governments and institutions by themselves in Africa. Thousands refuse to go, even when they may have freedom from American slavery by going. To the Africans, the thought of going to Africa is generally repugnant.

Is it not because the Almighty has, in His wisdom, designed it otherwise; and may He not hold that great continent yet in reserve, to be occupied by the posterity of Shem and Japheth, in connection with that of Ham?* .

From the record of God's dealings with the children of men, it no where nor at any time appears to be His design that any one class or condition of men should live by themselves, to the exclusion of all others. The rich and the poor, the learned and the ignorant, the white and the black, the good and the bad, are to abide together and be found in all communities; and in time the preserving, renewing, and life-giving principles of the Gospel will raise all to the full capacity of their being. Our Saviour said, "Ye have the poor with you always, and whensoever ye will ye may do them good, but me ye have not always." We know the good and bad dwell together. Our Lord, in his great prayer for those that believed on His name, said, "I pray not that thou shouldest take them out of the world, but that thou shouldest keep them from the evil." The young must not cast out the old, but are commanded to "rise up before the hoary head, and honor the person of the old man." It is God's plan that both abide together; that while the young are benefited by the wisdom, knowledge, and experience, by the *restraints, counsels*, and *examples* of the aged, they, in return, receive from the young, reverence, honor, comfort, and support. As it is ordained that these two strata of society, the upper and nether, should be mutually dependent on and beneficial to each other, so, may it not be ordered by God in His providence that the different branches of the human family shall, as masters and servants, be mutually dependent on each other for security, support, prosperity, comfort, and happiness? For the eternal salvation of the servant, it is not necessary that he should be the, or equal to the, master; in fact, his salvation is promoted by his abiding in the condition in which his lot has been cast, without discontent or rebellion. The master is not saved because he is master. It will not do for him to deny his responsibility, or neglect his duty to those

* Feeling interested in the prosperity of the colonization cause in Liberia, we endeavored, a few years since, to persuade an intelligent slave to accept of his freedom, on the condition that he would go to Africa under the auspices of the Colonization Society. We set before him all the advantages of going, even the chance that he might become the head of the colony, but he refused, and is still, if living, a bond servant, with the privilege of accepting the offer. The Colonization enterprise has failed, and, in all probability, will fail to the end, to enlist the affections, excite the interest, and attract to the colony the colored population of our country. But as a missionary enterprise for Africa, it has done great good, and is worthy of all support.

who serve him. So in regard to honor; by all good men the *faith-ful* servant will not be despised because he is a bond servant, but will be considered worthy of double honor, especially in the sight of God, who is no respecter of persons. The old couplet might be rendered thus :

> " Honor and shame from no condition rise ; •
> A Saviour receive, there the honor lies."

A few things might be said to men of consideration, in reference to that practical question of returning fugitive slaves, or persons bound to service, which some hold it is not our duty to do. The constitution under which we live makes it our imperative duty to return all fugitives.

This constitution is a solemn agreement, that received the assent of the original States, by the votes of the people, and of the additional States as they came into the Union.

The Constitution is not only the organic law of the land, but partakes of a nature higher than common law, viz., that of a treaty, or solemn covenant, between independent states or communities. To deliberately break any of the important provisions of such a covenant, is a breach of faith offensive to God as well as man. In the Scriptures, so profitable for our instruction, so able to make wise in the way of duty, we are taught, in the history of the Gibeonites, how God regards a broken treaty or covenant. It will be remembered that Joshua, the leader of Israel, on their entrance into the land of Canaan, did make, by the advice and consent of the elders of Israel, a treaty with the Gibeonites, descendants of Canaan, son of Ham, agreeing to spare and protect their lives (the only condition they seem to have required); Joshua and all Israel believing at the time that the Gibeonites were a far-off, distant nation, as they represented themselves to be, giving as evidence of the truth of their representations, their old clothes, worn-out shoes, musty bread, and old bottles of wine, which they said were all new when they left home. The account will be found in Joshua ix., where it states, further, that the treaty was made by the elders, without asking counsel of God. The treaty, however, being once made, the covenant-keeping God required Israel at the time to keep it, and afterward to perform its conditions, as we may learn from 2 Samuel xxi., when, more than four hundred years after the treaty was made, God sent a famine upon the children of Israel, year after year, for three years. King David, on inquiring of the Lord the cause of the famine, was informed that it was owing to the breaking of the treaty with the Gibeonites by his predecessor, King Saul, some of whom he had slain. Atonement or satisfaction was made, and the famine ceased.

If the unchangeable God looks with such displeasure upon the breaking of a treaty, made without His advice and counsel, with what anger must He regard us if we allow our Constitution to be broken in any of those important treaty stipulations between the different parties making it? If the Great Ruler of the universe, unexpectedly to the Gibeonites as well as Israelites, vindicated a treaty made without His counsel, may we not expect Him, in due time, to vindicate a Constitution and covenant agreement made by Washington and his associates, directed in the wisdom of God—for many in the celebrated convention that framed the Constitution believed in and sought counsel from God—besides tens of thousands who, in that day, sincerely prayed that the convention might be directed in wisdom. The hand of the Great Being, in whom are all our ways, is everywhere manifest in the history of our country. His ear was open, and He heard the petitions that went up in her behalf while the Constitution was being framed, and the result was an instrument seven times better than we had reason to expect from the wisest and best of men.

How truly the Almighty requires us to perform our word, may be learned from His own character. God is a spirit, and they that worship Him must do it in spirit and truth. The sincerity He requires in us toward himself, He requires in us toward each other, so that we have no right to break an agreement with our neighbor, in *deed* or *word;* not to defraud him in any way of his property, or accuse him of unrighteousness in that which we have allowed. "Blessed is he that sweareth to his hurt and changeth not." The command given to the Israelites, Ex. xxiii. 4, is still binding upon us in the letter and spirit of it : "If thou meet thine enemy's ox or ass going astray, thou shalt surely bring it back to him again."

But some contend for a "higher law" than the Constitution; made, they say, before it, and set at naught by it, and therefore they are not bound by the provisions of the Constitution to return fugitives, because it interferes with their "higher law," and contrary to it. The law of love requiring us "to do unto others what we would they should do unto us," is practically interpreted or rendered by the Abolitionist, "*to do unto others all that others may wish us to do unto them,*" which reduced to practice requires things absurd, ridiculous, and impossible. Criminals must go unpunished; the rich must give place to the poor; the high exchange conditions with the low; the learned and wise for the ignorant and foolish; kings must make way for their subjects; masters for their servants; white for black; an exchange for nationalities, races, and sexes, according as any might wish; and their interpretation of the higher law of love, if true and good, must govern in other worlds, and in all time to come. The golden rule is still the golden rule, and there is no difficulty with it, rightly understood and practiced. But we must not forget that the Highest of all requires, first of all, *justice* to others *before* *mercy* at the expense of others (as some are attempting), or even at their their expense.

It does not seem to have been any part of the mission of our Saviour to change the conditions of the human family (which are fixed by God), but to teach, rather, that in whatever condition we are, therewith to be content; and the effect of His Gospel, where received, is to raise immeasurably all conditions of men. There is no record that our Saviour stepped between or interfered with the king and his subject; with the officer and the soldier under his command, or that He ever set the servant against his master, or the poor against the rich, or one nation against another. He invited *all* men to come to Him and *amend* their lives, by the influence of the spirit He would impart to them; but everywhere He rebuked the proud and self-righteous, who thank God that they are better than other men; and will not come to Christ that they may have true life.

It must be admitted by all who receive the Scriptures as a perfect rule in precept and example, that St. Paul, the great Apostle who so abounded in revelations, had, beyond all others, such enlarged and comprehensive views of Gospel truth and duty, and was so endowed with its grace, wisdom, and spirit, that he must have fully and perfectly understood the requirements of the law and Gospel, including the so-called higher law. We may safely take St. Paul, after his conversion, more than any other man that ever lived, as a true exemplar of all that is holy in feeling and right in practice. Now, if St. Paul sent back (and there is no contro-. versy about the fact) to his master, Philemon Onesimus,* a runaway slave (or bond servant), and a Christian slave, too, for he was converted under St. Paul's preaching after he had run away, we may go and do likewise without being charged with evil. The Lord may rebuke us if we accuse of sin those who imitate the Apostle in this matter, thereby setting our righteousness above St.

* Onesimus means, in the original, "profitable." It is said that not long after his return to his master, he was sent back again to Rome, that he might be of service to St. Paul in his prison.

Paul's, flattering ourselves that we comprehend the true teachings of the Gospel more perfectly than the great Apostle, who was taught by Jesus Christ himself.

A few words in regard to that other question—the right of the master to take his bond-servants into new territories, not yet organized into States. On what right is his claim based? The Constitution allows the citizens of every State, at their will and pleasure, to settle in any territory belonging to the government. There are no restrictions in the Constitution on this point. No citizen of any class, condition, or State is prohibited from settling in the Territories, taking all his substance the:.., and making it his home. Besides that, it is an important and acknowledged principle in our Constitution and government, that laws and measures unequal in their effects or requirements on citizens or sections are not to be enacted, or allowed to stand on any common or national ground.

What are the primitive or natural rights of man in the premises? The inspired King David writes: "The heavens are the Lord's, but the earth hath He given to the children of men." The prophet Isaiah writes: "God formed the earth and made it; He hath established it; He created it not in vain; He formed it *to be inhabited.*" In Genesis it is recorded that when the government and possession of the earth was turned over to man, the condition or command was, go forth, replenish, and subdue the earth. Let the ten thousand varied resources of the earth be discovered, developed, and brought into subjection to various uses of man and to the glory of the Creator. This original command came down to Noah and his children; it has not been repealed, but is still binding on the human family, and the greater part of the world is still waiting for man to fulfill the condition of the original charter. The command has come down through the generations to us, and is not limited to any particular race or condition of the human family. All whose circumstances will admit, have the right to go forth into the unsettled portions of the earth and inhabit them. The rich and the poor, the master and his servant, may go and settle in the land, organize governments, and make laws consistent with righteousness. They are God's territories, still held in reserve for man, and inviting him to develop their untold resources. All the natural and conferred rights of citizens will be protected by every good government, at home and abroad.

The question may be asked and considered, Why has little or no progress been made for a whole generation toward removing or bringing to an end the system of slavery, as it is called, in our country? There are now more States where this system is allowed, and more than one third more Africans held as bond-servants, than there was thirty years ago. If this great system of bond-servants was the result of the counsels and work of men alone, it would have long since come to naught. Have we not reason to conclude that it exists by the righteous will as well as permission of God? There is not any great missionary or benevolent enterprise, of which we have any knowledge, but that has accomplished a great work in the past ten, not to say thirty years. But in this work of overthrowing or removing from our land the "peculiar institution" of African servitude, nothing has been accomplished.

The multitude of prayers that have been offered up (without the condition, "If it be thy will, O Lord!"); the thousands of influences and the unceasing efforts of tens and hundreds of thousands of ardent and zealous people, have all failed to remove this condition of bondage from even the smallest of the States in which it exists. The fierce winds that have blown upon it have tended only to make it take deeper root where it exists, and like the old oak, it stands stronger to-day than ever. The main question of this day is, Shall this system be allowed or prevented from establishing itself in the Territories? and sooner or later the answer of the public will be, Let it go where it will. How unexpected to many that the result of so much effort, vain confidence, and boasting should be, that not a step has been taken toward the legal emancipation of a single slave! But "Who is he that saith and it cometh to pass, when the Lord commandeth not?"*

The general expectation at the North thirty years ago was, that soon all, or nearly all, the States would abolish slavery, and a prominent question in the minds of many seemed to be, which State would first voluntarily remove the condition of bondage from the Africans. Now, voluntary emancipation is hardly thought of in any State; and those at the North who once expected to accomplish all that they desired on that principle, have abandoned that

---

* Somewhere about the year 1836, thirty dollars was handed to a gentleman of this city to make a lady in the country a life-member of the American Home Missionary Society, but from some misunderstanding he applied to the American Anti-Slavery Society for the certificate of life-membership for the donor. The secretary of the Society replied that they had no life-membership established. The gentleman stated that he must have a certificate, or he could not leave the money. The secretary, rising from his chair, and pacing his office in an excited manner, said, "Why, sir, a life-membership is the last thing thought of; in a few years we are confident that most of the slave States will abolish slavery, and in ten years at the farthest all will have emancipation laws passed, and then there would be no further use for the American Anti-Slavery Society."

idea, and many of them have put their reliance on the god of forces, and have attracted to themselves a strong political organization, who are glad to use this Abolition element to place themselves in power and affluence, and at the same time by outnumbering forces, unfriendly measures, and violent efforts of some kind, separate the servant from his master, and destroy the influence, power, and value of the institution wherever it exists, the accomplishment of which would suit the feelings of zealous Abolitionists, although master and servant would be involved in ruin!

The citizens of the South, among whom this system of bond-service prevails, have less and less faith in the so-called blessings of emancipation; have more fear of the evils resulting from such an act, see vividly the suffering, danger, and ruin following to the whites and blacks, so that they feel it is a duty they owe to themselves and to their servants, to resist every influence used in any way, directly or indirectly, to bring about emancipation. They consider also that all influences and efforts put forth to weaken or destroy the "institution of bond-servants," as a- invasion of their rights, and a manifest determination on the part of others to overthrow it as soon as possible, even in opposition to the sentiment of the community in which it exists. The citizens of the South consider that they are the best judges of what most affects their rights and institutions, and know best what ought and ought not to be done; that in self-defense they are bound to oppose all efforts made against them, whether they be acts of omission or commission, holding that they are contrary to the spirit and letter of the Constitution, and do in fact break the bonds of the Union, and therefore they are no longer bound to the Union, but have perfect right and liberty to withdraw and set up an independent government, that they might more effectually perfect measures to protect and defend themselves from all enemies, which they are able to do, many to the contrary notwithstanding. The Union is dear to the South, but their rights, homes, and institutions are dearer to them than the Union of these States. All who are engaged in this irrepressible conflict (God did not raise it, and He can repress it), in driving on this sectional contest, ought to pause, and consider calmly the real effect of their opinions, words, and acts, before it is too late. They profess to be moved by good and righteous motives in all that they do, and it is a solemn duty they owe to themselves, to the South, and to the world, to show and make manifest their authority for their acts and opinions, the doing and holding of which cause so much trouble and distress in the world. They ought not only to explain away the judicial sentence of servitude pronounced by God upon the descendants of Ham, as found in Gen. ix., and all other passages favoring that condition of servitude in the Old Testament, together with the example of good and holy men that bought and held servants in bondage, but they ought to bring from the Old Testament some text, saying, Thus saith the Lord, thou shalt not buy nor hold bond men or women; and from the New Testament they ought to prove, from the teachings and example of our Lord and His Apostles, that they disapproved, censured, and condemned the then prevalent practice of holding bond men and women in a state of servitude. If they can not do this, they ought to wait, and let God speak first before they condemn others. God is either wholly for or wholly against this institution of bond-servants; if the latter, He will in his providence pull it down and remove it from the face of the earth. If He is for it, as we believe His truth and providence make it manifest He is, then He will build it up and establish it, and in due time cause to cease all the assaults of its enemies, and make the world to behold the institution in its true proportions, and appreciate and desire its blessings. The institution finds support not only in God's Word and providence, but also in the practical experience, common sense, and judgment of large and intelligent communities for generations, in which the principles of the Gospel have and do prevail. It has been and is still supported by Christian men, who, with a good conscience, hold servants in bondage, and still make it manifest to all around that they are true disciples of the Saviour, for they show the mark and bear the test given by Him, " by their fruits shall ye know them."

We do not perceive the wisdom or truth of the saying recorded in Proverbs by the wisest of men, that " he that is despised and hath a servant is better than he that honoreth himself and lacketh bread," unless it is understood that the servant mentioned is a bond and not a hired servant. If the Almighty has made servitude the judicial law for the posterity of Ham, we must not think that we can in any way cheat Him, or prevent the execution of the sentence; servitude will still be the law for the descendant of Ham; and if he has not one permanent master, as at the South, for whom he may labor, and in whom he may trust and feel secure, he will have to be subject to many masters, as at the North, and keenly feel his unprotected and dependent condition.

A few days since an intelligent negro man was complaining of his hard lot. He was industrious, a good mechanic, and competent for most any work, yet he said he could not get employment in any store, factory, or mechanic's shop in the city. He was willing to work, but could not earn money enough to buy bread for his wife and three children; they had to beg. "Nothing but his cursed black skin," he said, "prevented him from having a competence." Just such a man, under the institution, would be appreciated and honored, and find his true place; and his master, like Abraham of old, might give him charge over all that he had. Does any one think, that because this man was free, that he escaped the law of his race—servitude? Under pretense of doing a favor, *how cruel* it is to oust one out of his true place, and then leave him dependent on the cold charities of the world! This institution of bond-servants meets exactly, in every point of view, the wants of the whites and blacks, showing that it must have been designed by some one wiser than man. It is happily adapted to the natural, religious, and social wants and feelings of both races. It is probably the worst slandered institution in the world; but there are no evils connected with it but what are either common to the lot of man, or that can be removed by proper laws, regulations, and conduct. If the great public who have formed an opinion adverse to it would refrain from denying any good in it, and for a time withhold their prejudices until they could consider it calmly and fairly in all its relations and results, they would soon find more to commend than to condemn.

From what we have observed and know to be facts, we firmly believe the bond-servants of the South enjoy as great a measure of happiness as falls to the lot of any other laboring people on the globe. Their necessary wants, few and simple, are all supplied, and their comfort and happiness in a good measure considered. They have a degree of contentment that is surprising; they feel secure, and are delivered from the care-worm that so eats at the vitals of all happiness. It is singular what simple and honest faith the great body of the negroes have in God and in His Word, what delight they have in His worship,* and love and respect for His ministers.

* The *Journal of Commerce* lately published a letter, written by the wife of a minister of the Gospel, residing in Mississippi: "You know, my dear friend, I speak from experience, when I tell you of the slave here in his far Southern home. 'Tis long years that my home has been cast among them in this sunny clime, and as I have loved my own New England home, so do I love this, the home of my adoption; I love not only my home, but the dear people around us. Some noble specimens of the Christian we meet here, both among the high and lowly of the land. Here are noble, self-sacrificing Christian slaveholders, actuated by Christianity in all that they do. I wish all were Christians; but, alas! here, as elsewhere, mammon too often binds the soul down to earth. The slaves around us gladly hear the Word, and seem to be pressing into the kingdom; of course not all; many care for none of these things. But on all the plantations around us there are many pious, devoted, praying Christians; could you hear their prayers and songs of praise, as I do often, when I accompany my husband

27

If they are in trouble or distress, they would risk their lives for them, as the Ethiopian did who saved the life of the prophet Jeremiah.

In the towns they have liberty given by most masters to worship where they please—the master going to one church and the servant to the same, or any other, as he thinks best. Hundreds of thousands of these bond-servants are made to rejoice in the liberty of the Gospel and freedom from the bondage of sin, by the blessing of God, not on the efforts of those who sought to deliver them from His sentence of servitude, but on the humble labors of those who, in the spirit of their Master in heaven, sought to do them good, through evil as well as good report; and though their labors may have been unnoticed, and considered of no account by the great public, yet they have the satisfaction of knowing that they are appreciated by the confiding and grateful negro, having the assurance, also, that their Father in heaven smiles upon and blesses them. They may know, also, that there are more than ten times seven thousand at the North who believe that the faithful master is a true Christian, and delight to own and call him brother; although many among us are too righteous to commune or hold fellowship with him!

It is the glory of the Gospel that it is adapted to and meets the wants of all classes and conditions of men everywhere on the habitable globe; none are too high or too low. All are included within its call, and its provisions are full and free and all-sufficient. Who, then, shall limit this Gospel, or the grace of God, by asserting that He is not as able and willing to grant salvation to the bond servant as to his master, or any other man? Shall we say that the High God, who "regards with favor the lowly,"

to the different plantations, where he regularly preaches, it would do your heart good. My husband has access to some nine or ten plantations, where, Sabbath after Sabbath, he expounds the pure Gospel of Christ to this interesting race ; I assure you they hear him gladly. They grasp the great truths of our religion with an avidity and clearness that would surprise you. These simple, trusting creatures know no better way than just to take God at His word, and believe what He says. And then, their prayers are as orthodox as those of our old New England fathers were. They pray for the advance of Christ's kingdom, for themselves, their masters—many of them God-forgetting men. Often, too, their masters I have seen standing right in their midst, by the side of the minister, while these fervent petitions were going to God in their behalf. Must not such prayers be good? Surely, if nothing more, it must bind together the master and slave in bonds of love. But such fervent, simple, heartfelt prayers God will hear. But when they pray for their pastor, then, truly, they become eloquent. I weep, and they are tears of thankfulness, that there are those who so fervently pray for him. They are so grateful that he will come and break to them the bread of life. I believe God hears their prayers, and gives my husband strength to labor on."

though "no respecter of persons," will, or does, make the condition of labor or service (in which *per se* there is no sin) a barrier to eternal life through His Son? May it not be His glory to make His grace "much more abound" to all who are under this condition of servitude.

May not the descendants of Ham, by obedience to the "commandment which was ordained to bondage," find it to be to them eternal freedom, and in the end acknowledge with joy that the commandment was just and good?

If this be so, their resistance or murmuring against the commandment of their life operates against their acceptance of the Gospel, and is one reason why the proportion of free black Christians at the North is less than those at the South. A gentleman from the South who has all his days been living amid and conversant with the blacks, informed us the past season that he never yet came across one that held infidel sentiments. It is not altogether so here; some, like Fred. Douglas, are worse than infidels.

It is the general opinion of the great body of those opposed to African servitude in our country, that all abolition and emancipation doctrines and practices have their foundation in and proceed from the New Testament. But they may search that Book in vain to prove their doctrines and practices good and righteous. Let them follow the pages of history down to the period of the French infidel revolution in 1790, and they will then behold a great outburst of Abolition sentiment and spirit. Then fanatics and infidels ruled the hour, crying out that "there was no God;" "Death was an eternal sleep," proclaiming Liberty, Fraternity, and Equality for the white and black. They embraced and kissed negroes, whom they admitted to their National Assembly, which political body soon set free, without compensation, more than 300,000 savage blacks in the Island of St. Domirgo, many of them recently imported from Africa. These were all suddenly set loose on thirty or forty thousand defenseless whites, who were barbarously massacred, their dwellings burned, property destroyed, and the island left desolate, from which it has not recovered to this day.

From the French Revolution to this present time there has been more or less infidelity, fanaticism, world-religion, and spirit of self-righteous and fashionable reform mixed up with the whole question in this country and England, all aiming to accomplish just one object, the emancipation of the negro; then their mission would be filled, and they would not be bound to do anything more for him!

May not some good men of the present day be as much mistaken in the idea that the Gospel calls for and demands the freedom and equality of the blacks, as the disciples were that its success required the restoration in great splendor of kingdom and power to the Jews?

Those who oppose the institution and seek to emancipate the African from the condition of servitude, propose no wise or feasible plan for his provision after he is emancipated (which is all important to the African), neither have they any good place or home to offer him on the face of the earth. Read what the New York *Courier and Enquirer* published August 3d, as a brief synopsis of the Republican creed, the following of which is the sixth article, although the editor says it is not generally avowed.

" *Sixth.* The negro, in our judgment, is physically, socially, and morally in a better condition as a slave, in most of the slave States, than he would be in a state of freedom ; and therefore, opposed as we are to the institution, if the General Government possessed the power and the constitutional right to abolish slavery in the slave States, we should earnestly protest against its abolition without first providing for the extradition of the freed man beyond the limits of the United States."

We have no dissent to make to the first part of the article, but would ask, If the negro is better off as a slave, why make such strenuous efforts to set him free? and if freed, to what civilized country could you send him outside of these States, as you say he must go? If to Africa you send him, on what principle of love or good-will can you send him back to the dangers of heathen barbarism? Your doctrines will not stand the various tests that wisdom, truth, and righteousness demand.

If we go back for two hundred years and study the history of this system of servitude in a pecuniary point of view—the lowest point to view it—we will be surprised at its effects and results on the trade and commerce of the world, and how much it has done to increase the wealth of all civilized nations. In the 16th century, before the civilized world began to reap the benefit of African labor on the rich soils of America, England, France, and the European nations were comparatively poor, but since the fruit of their labor has been turned in upon them, the commerce of the world has felt more and more the quickening impulses of it, and wealth in great abundance has accumulated in England, America, and other nations, mostly the result of their labor. The annual product of African slave labor is estimated at over $500,000,000, produced by some 6,000,000 of blacks, more than one half of which is from the United States.

This system has added more to the wealth and independence of
our country than any other interest in it. Even the North, by its
trade and intercourse with the South, has increased a vast deal
more its wealth and prosperity than it has by its trade with any
other section or country. Let those who doubt this investigate the
matter thoroughly to the end in every branch of trade and business,
and they will be satisfied that the statement is true.

It is well to inquire how emancipation has worked where it has
been tried. A wise man will try no costly experiments, when he
may, from the experience of others, learn just what is necessary for
him to know.

If for a lesson we look to the island of St. Domingo, once the
most flourishing and prosperous island on the globe, we will find,
as the result of emancipation there, that the island is, to all intents
and purposes, lost to the civilized world. France owes it to herself, humanity, and the world to reclaim it. Much was expected
from emancipation in the British West India Islands. The result
was observed with much interest by those for and against the
measure in our country, as well as in England; and there seemed
at the time to be a sort of tacit understanding, that if the measure
worked well and for the good of all concerned, then the work of
abolishing involuntary servitude would go on; but if it was
otherwise, then Abolitionists would cease all active efforts to bring
about a general emancipation.

That that work of emancipation in the British West India Islands has proved a complete failure, is now admitted by every man
of common information and sense. Those once rich and prosperous islands are now impoverished, and on "the verge of social
barbarism." The richly freighted commercial ships that used to
crowd their ports are seen no more.

Read what Mr. Anthony Trollope (an avowed emancipationist),
in his work on the West India Islands, lately published by Harper
& Bros., says: "That Jamaica was a land of wealth, rivaling
the East in its riches, nay, excelling it as a market for its
capital; as a place in which money might be turned, and that it
is now a spot on the earth almost more poverty-stricken than any
other, so much is known almost to all men. That this change
was brought about by the manumission of the slaves, which was com-
pleted in 1838—of that, also, the English world is generally aware.

"Englishmen well know that half of the sugar estates in Jamaica,
and I believe more than half of the coffee plantations, have gone
back into a state of bush. That all this land, rich with the
richest produce some thirty years since, has now fallen back into

wilderness—that the world hereabouts has so retrograded—that chaos and darkness have re-swallowed so vast an extent of the most beautiful land that civilization had ever mastered, and that, too, beneath the British Government. Property has been abandoned as good for nothing, and nearly forgotton, or sold for what worthless trifle it would fetch. And of those who are now growing canes in Jamaica, a great portion are gentlemen who have lately bought their estates for the value of the copper in the sugar boilers, and if to this has been added anything like a fair value for wheels in the machinery, the estate has not been badly sold."

Are we anxious to try any such costly experiments? Mr. Trollope thus speaks of the negro, and the effect that emancipation there has had upon him:

"Without a desire for property, man could make no progress. But the negro has no such desire; no desire to induce him to labor for that which he wants. In order that he may eat to-day and be clothed to-morrow he will work a little; as for anything beyond that, he is content to lie in the sun. To recede from civilization and become again savage, as savage as the laws of the community can permit, has been to his taste. I believe that he would altogether retrograde if left to himself."

There is no doubt of it; the race has not and can not stand alone in an elevated position, any. more than the vine can without the tree.

Mr. Trollope says further, that " the negro idea of emancipation was and is, emancipation, not from slavery, but from work. To lie in the sun and eat bread-fruit and yams is his idea of being free. Such freedom as that has not been intended for man in this world; and I say, as Jamaica now exists, is still under a *devil's ordinance.* It would be well if we could so contrive that he should not eat or live without work. It is clearly not nature's intention that he should be exempted from the general lot of Adam's children."

These stubborn facts, that won't lie and can not be put down, bear hard upon the doctrines of Abolitionists, of which Mr. Trollope is one. Let us see how he reconciles facts with favorite theories:

" Having said so much, I shall now be asked," he says, " whether I think emancipation was wrong ? By no means; I think emancipation was clearly right. For, thinking as we did, that slavery was a sin, from that sin we have cleared ourselves. But the mere fact of doing so has not freed us from our difficulties. Nor was it expected that it should. The discontinuance of sin is always the commencement of a struggle."

Fudge! Whenever we put our will and wisdom against the will of God, and seek to have our plans (no matter how benevolent they may appear) supersede the Word and providential designs of the Almighty, we are sure to run into inextricable difficulties. One fault of these great reformers was and is, that their benevolence exceeds the goodness, and their plans the wisdom, of God.

Perhaps many will be surprised when we ask the question, What has New England and her colored population gained by emancipation, the section of all others in our Union where the institution, it would seem, was least wanted?

The African population there, instead of gaining in numbers, have decreased largely, in comparison with the colored population of the South. This increase of population is a good and true test and proof of physical well-being, comfort, and happiness. Neither can it be said that the African population of New England have made any progress, or that advancement in religion and morals, in the mechanical arts and agricultural pursuits, in habits of industry and economy, in exemption from poverty and crime, that was hoped for and expected. Those that are left are still servants according to God's judgment, free indeed from one master, but, as a rule, dependent on many masters, without the certainty of any caring for their spiritual or temporal wants, or providing them with necessary labor and sustenance.

The great sources of wealth, prosperity, and happiness to any people are the various products of their soil. The soil on which we live, labor, and thrive is God's capital loaned to men, which He has promised to water by His rains, and warm into life by the heat of His sun, that it may certainly yield to man its annual interest in return for his labor invested in it.

It is man's duty not to let the soil idle that God has loaned him, but to invest the labor he can control into it.

In amount and value of agricultural products, in comparison with former years and population, New England has greatly depreciated. We think, on investigation, it will be found that the breadth of land tilled is much less than it formerly was. In almost every section of it there are hundreds and thousands of acres lying idle, some of which is still in its original wilderness condition. A great part of the best farming lands are laid down or "gone to grass," simply because that crop requires the least labor and expense to handle, although it may be the least in value. The recent and former census show that, while the manufacturing towns have increased, the population in the farming and rural districts has decreased. It is the natural desire of man to remain and settle at or near the home of his youth; but New England presents so few inducements to her industrious and enterprising young men, that a host of them are obliged to look and go outside of her for subsistence and wealth. That class of men are the hope and strength of any State, and it is a poor consolation for New England to know that they thrive well elsewhere. This ought not to be so. We can not believe that the Almighty intended it should be so. The sons should grow up with the fathers—the young with the old. There must be some mistake somewhere, and if there is, rest assured that it is with us and not with God.

The main dependence of New England and sources of her wealth at present are to be found in her commercial, mechanical, and manufacturing interests, most of which are engaged in and for the Southern market. It should not be forgotten, that those interests can not long or well thrive, unless those engaged in them are well and cheaply fed. No section or people can afford to be entirely dependent on others for the principal articles of subsistence. Even the Golden State did not really prosper till they raised their own provisions, of which they have now become exporters. "Agriculture in its various branches must form the basis of the prosperity and power of the American people." "It is the great foundation of our national wealth and consequence."

What New England most wants at this time to make her farming interest worth double, if not triple, its present value is, that her farmers should be supplied permanently with able, steady, reliable, and cheap laborers, who would feel a growing interest in the prosperity of the farm, and who would be more under the control of the owner of it. With a supply of such laborers on her soil, which is sweet, and, on the whole, of good quality, her farming lands would soon greatly increase in value—her waste and wild lands would be reclaimed—her half-cultivated fields be well tilled—and the hundreds of thousands of acres left year after year to bear a scanty crop of grass, could be made to bring forth abundant and profitable crops of that which the community and the world require. Hemp and flax might be made to grow again in her fields; flocks of sheep feed on her hills and beside her streams; and the silk-worm cultivated with success. Then her population would increase and more of it be retained on her soil. Her farmers might make their tens, fifties, and hundreds of thousands (as farmers or planters do in other sections of our land). They would rise to men of patriarchal position, importance, and influence, and ability to do good to others; an air of ease, comfort, and happiness everywhere abound.

A prudent farmer will be slow to start any new enterprise or plan more work than he can well perform himself, for he knows in these days that dependence on hired labor is precarious, unreliable, and expensive; that most of the temporary hired laborers care not for the farm, the crop, or the owner, but seek large pay for little labor, and oft are more apt to leave in the midst of the harvest than any other time. The experienced farmer knows well that change — this incessant change—change of laborers, indoors and out—is pernicious to his interest, and opposed to the thrift, comfort, and happiness of himself and family.

Is it not remarkable that the unceasing efforts of the civilized world fail to break up entirely the slave trade? With reason, we might think it would be much harder to drive the pirates back from every sea through which so many defenseless, yet richly laden, ships are ever sailing, and offer to the pirate an easy prize; but for more than two generations the pirate's vessel has not been found, or hardly known. It must be notorious to every well-informed person, that at this time there are many more slave vessels of America, as well as of other nationalities, engaged upon the Atlantic in transporting Africans to America than have been known before for a score of years. Even steamers, it is reported, are now employed in the business, and the efforts and laws of nations seem to be a nullity. Why, then, do the efforts of France, England, and America fail to prevent what they have declared to be piracy, and denominated an abominable traffic—this transporting Africans from the land of cruelty and heathen darkness across the ocean to labor for men of another race, to the benefit of the civilized world, and their own temporal and eternal welfare? Why do the efforts of the most powerful goveroments of the world fail in the accomplishment of this darling object of their ambition, unless it is because they are endeavoring (though ignorantly) to thwart the righteous designs of the Almighty? The wise man tells us in Ecclesiastes : "Consider the work of God; for who can make that straight which He hath made crooked?"

Who shall say that this may not be God's plan, in the present state of the world, of introducing the poor African to civilization and the knowledge of the Gospel? If it should be, we can not overthrow it; our efforts would end in our confusion, for we would be found fighting against God.

We do not and can not justify or palliate the unnecessary hardships and cruelties of the middle-passage. But the dangers and sufferings endured on the voyage of transportation are not necessarily connected with this commerce of labor. It must be evident to all, that most of these evils grow out of efforts made by the violators of the public law or policy to escape from the powerful and systematic plans adopted by the nations to break up and prevent this commerce of labor. If the powers of Great Britain and Germany should make the same efforts on the ocean to prevent the migration of their citizens to our country, we should hear of and witness like results.

The expensive and gigantic efforts of the nations to prevent this traffic have signally failed, and will continue to fail. England alone has spent over $200,000,000 since 1820 to put an end to this commerce, but without avail. Would it not be better, then, to legalize this most natural supply of this continual demand of the civilized world for more laborers ?*

By the appointment of proper government agents at the places of embarkation, to see that violence was not used and vessels in proper condition, and that the transportation of the Africans should be made in good vessels, under the laws and subject to the same control and regulations that govern our most approved emigrant ships, then the migratory voyage *per se* could me made with little or no suffering.

The whole world is fast being opened to civilization, trade, and commerce, and everywhere there is a growing desire to develop the inexhaustible resources of the world, that the Creator is fast revealing to the astonished inhabitants of the earth, as if the people felt resting upon them the original injunction or command of the Almighty, to subdue the earth and bring everything in it to the use and good of man and glory of the Creator. Consequently, there comes up from the civilized world a continual cry for laborers—or demand for the labor of those who are able to dig in the earth, to develop its resources or bring forth its products. This natural demand will somehow be met ; obstructions thrown in the way will be as powerless to prevent as any that could be thrown to stop Niagara in its course to the ocean.

The most powerful of all obstacles has been, and is, public opinion, that seems to be giving way ; and now the common mind does not look upon the matter with that horror that many think they ought, therefore are slow to convict and punish those who have offended against the law. As we use the reservoirs of coal bountifully provided by the Creator to keep alive the fires of civilization, why may we not go to the great reservoirs of laborers existing in Africa, and accept the services of those who have been through the ages standing idle, and worse than idle, because none would

* The *Journal of Commerce* of September 14th says, that " slaves will make their way to Havana as surely as cotton to England."

employ and use them to aid in performing the necessary labor of civilization.

The coal and the laborers alike belong to God: the one He has given to the inhabitants of the earth; the other, in His righteous judgment, He has turned over to the descendants of Shem and Japheth, blessing them with the service of Ham's posterity.

The condition of native Africans on that continent is dreadful to contemplate. According to the account of the Rev. Mr. Lindley, a missionary of the American Board of Commissioners for Foreign Missions, who has lately returned from Southeastern Africa, in which section he has been laboring for a number of years, we learn that the Africans are, and have been for ages, sunk to the lowest degree of degradation that it is possible to conceive of beyond hope of self-recovery. They live in a naked condition, without comforts, in small huts, the entrance to which is only two or three feet high, and which entrance is the only place for the smoke of their fires to escape. They sleep at night in these huts, crowded with human beings, sheep, goats, and dogs, all mixed together. The negro men are barbarous, cruel, and lazy, and treat each other, especially the women, with great severity. With a few head of cattle the men purchase their wives, of which they have half a dozen or more. The women are compelled by the men to do all the work.

The accounts of this missionary are perfectly reliable, although painfully interesting, giving us, as they do, an idea of the moral death that reigns over that continent beyond the conception of any one, white or black, that lives in this Gospel land. The negro, without the Gospel, and left to himself, tends downward all the time. Mr. Lindley said that the *power of example* had more influence in bringing them up to a state of semi-civilization than anything else. The great traveler, Park, states that three fourths of the inhabitants of Africa (the descendants of Ham) are in wretched slavery.

It is high time that the darkness of that continent was penetrated and its dark host scattered among the nations, where they could be made useful to others and happy themselves. The annual waste, and worse than waste, of human life and labor on the continent of Africa* could, by a proper and well-regulated system of

* The following extract from the *West African Herald*, of July 13th, will give an idea of the cruelty and condition of the Africans. Late accounts state that this horrible custom was duly performed. The Africans in our Southern States are in a paradise in comparison with those left in Africa.

"His Majesty Radahung, King of Dahomey, is about to make the 'Grand Cus-

imi iigration to civilized lands, be stopped, and, instead, be made to become a living and self-supplying source of wealth to the nations, in the enjoyments and fruits of which the laborers would share. Coming in contact with practical civilization, learning important truths concerning body and soul, they could not but be greatly benefited, and in the end acknowledge that it was more blessed to give or render service than to receive it, and would themselves soon embrace every opportunity of coming to this land. This plan, so beneficial to all concerned, would be readily set in motion and kept in operation if we would not interfere, but allow natural causes to work. Would it not be more wise, humane, and Christian to allow this plan to operate, than for us to adopt the policy of the dog in the manger—neither receive the laborers nor allow others to receive and use them, though the world would be benefited? England, in some respects wiser than we are, confesses to the value of African labor, in that she sends all her captured Africans to be apprenticed in her colonies, while we return them to Africa. If the exodus of the tillers of the soil from Great Britain should continue for a few years, England herself, under some proper system of apprenticeship, will be glad to receive the services of the Africans. Our government, last spring, sent back to the west coast of Africa some two thousand negroes, at an expense of nearly $300,000. Would not the wise and true Christian course have been, to have sent the poor negroes to some of our Northern ports and apprenticed them out to farmers, to whom they would have been of great service, and from whom, by example and precept, they might have learned the truths of the Gospel?

If Japheth wants the service of Ham, and he is willing to submit himself to the will and control of Japheth, and render him service, it is neither wise nor good to put obstructions in the way, or prevent what may be a natural relation or condition of things, and which experience, so far as it has been tried, proves to be good for both Ham and Japheth.

If we take our Constitution, and judge from its provisions and

tom' in honor of the late King Gezo. Determined to surpass all former monarchs in the magnitude of his ceremonies to be performed on this occasion, Badahung has made the most extensive preparations for the celebration of the 'Grand Custom.' A great pit has been dug which is to contain human blood enough to float a canoe. Two thousand persons will be sacrificed on this occasion. The expedition to Abeakeuta is postponed, but the king has sent his army to make some excursions at the expense of some weaker tribes, and has succeeded in capturing many unfortunate creatures. The young people among these prisoners will be sold into slavery, and the old persons will be killed at the 'Grand Custom.' "

phraseology, we will decide that the framers of it were opposed to any prohibition of the slave trade. In the Constitution we find no prohibition whatever to the slave trade, or importing laborers from Africa or elsewhere. In fact, it *prohibits* the *stoppage* of all such business prior to the year 1808, and after that period allows Congress, as they may think best, to put an end to, or continue the business. It is the general opinion that the great instrument prohibits the trade after 1808, that it can not now be opened only by a change in the Constitution, requiring a vote of three fourths of the people in its favor. Those who will take the trouble to investigate the matter will find that it is not so. What is more singular still, and what seems a providential interposition in behalf of some native Africans, is that clause in the Constitution directing how and what changes might be made in that instrument, which in a particular manner guards the right to import laborers up to the year 1808, and allows three fourths of the people to pull down the framework of government, and change every part of the Constitution, excepting the immigration or importation of bond-servants, which they must not touch. Congress since that period has used the power conferred on it—has prohibited this commerce of labor—declared it to be and affixed to it the penalties of piracy. It is one thing to call evil good, and good evil, and quite another to make them so. Congress can not make a thing good or sinful, only so far as conforming to or breaking the act of Congress is good or sinful. We may inquire if the death penalty affixed to this traffic is constitutional? The eighth article of the amendments of the Constitution reads thus: "Excessive bail shall not be required, nor excessive fines imposed, nor cruel and unusual punishments inflicted."

What is the meaning of the latter part of this article? When the Constitution was made, and long after, the transportation of Africans from that continent to ours was considered right by many, and was no crime in the eye of any law on our statute books; the inflicting, then, the death penalty for the mere breaking, not the law of God, not an article of our Constitution, but an act of Congress, is both cruel and unusual, therefore unconstitutional. Some, perhaps, may say the article refers to the form or instrument used—that to be guillotined, instead of hung, is cruel and unusual. Gammon! In this instance we think the death penalty is unconstitutional, and unjust when the owner and master of the transporting vessel *cares and provides well* for the lives and comfort of the immigrants committed to them; but if they neglect both of these important matters, and manifest a disregard for life, then they ought to be hung or guillotined.

When it is remembered that we are commanded—Lev. xxv. 44—
to buy our bond-servants, not of each other, but of the heathen, for
the obvious reason that their condition would then be immeasurably bettered, where can we go but to the great reservoir in Africa?
And regarding this institution as stated in these pages, there is no
other way but to recommend the removing of all restrictions on
this foreign commerce of labor, and the establishing of it upon an
enlightened and liberal basis.

Let us stand where our fathers stood. Let us step back upon the
platform of practical wisdom, made by the Governor of the world,
and fenced in by His truth and providence. Shall we do evil, that
good may come? No. Shall we refrain from doing good, lest evil
may come? No. Is truth, one of God's attributes, ever consistent
with itself? Always. Is mercy, and all of God's attributes, ever
consistent with themselves and each other? Always. God is ever
consistent with Himself. Rest assured, that in all His providential
dealings with man, He will never allow His providential works to
operate against the gracious designs of His love and mercy. His
providences may sometimes to us, and even to angels, appear dark
and inexplicable, but the end will be light, salvation, and glory.
We may safely adopt the principle and rule, as mentioned in the
preceding pages, *that whatever is best for the spiritual interest of
any man, and will most promote his eternal salvation, is right for
us to do, and in perfect accordance with the will and character of
the Almighty.* Now then, if retaining in our Gospel land Africans
captured on the ocean by our national vessels, or if, by sending
vessels to Africa, we may peaceably induce them to leave their land
of darkness and death and come to this land, where the means of
life so abound and mercy can lay hold on them, is it not our duty to
keep them when here, or allow them to come or bring them here?
Shall we refuse to do them a good act—to place them where they
will be more useful and happy for time, and where their eternal
happiness may be secured? If we apprehend and say some evils
will surely arise from such acts on our part, will not Mercy be true
to herself, and provide a way of escape for all apprehended evils?

If some say that such a course is contrary to God's truth, or His
plans of mercy, let them prove it.

If we can prove that the salvation of a multitude of souls (the
grand design God ever keeps in view) is greatly advanced or secured by such a course of action on our part, we may rest assured
that it is right. Some may reply, that those engaged in bringing
heathen Africans over to this country, do it from motives of gain
only, therefore it ought not to be allowed. We know that our

motives must be pure and right before they can find acceptance with the great Judge, and He is the only proper one to judge the motives of our conduct. With Him we must all stand or fall. But still, there is a principle on which it may be allowed, laid down by the Apostle Paul in his letter to the Philippians, when he states that "some preach Christ through envy, strife, and contention; others from love and good will. What, then?" he says, "notwithstanding, every way, whether in pretense, or in truth, Christ is preached; and I do therein rejoice, yea, and will rejoice."

We are never to forget that our African bond-servants have souls that are precious and must be cared for. We must feel our responsibility like a father or guardian, and 'that, while we serve ourselves of them, take care for our own sakes as well as theirs, that we do not offend or lead them astray, for their angels do behold the face of their Father in heaven, who will avenge them.

The family is an institution from God; considered in all its relations, it is the happiest in the world. Families that are governed in the fear and love of God are everywhere little fountains of blessings. In every family, properly organized, a servant or servants seem to be indispensable to its comfort and happiness. This must be apparent to every one. If servants are necessary for the family, God knows it, and has provided for it. He provides for all our necessary wants. He overrules events and adapts means to accomplish His ends. His own institution, the family, would be provided for; He would make it complete in all its appointments. We believe he has met this necessity in the families of Shem and Japheth, by giving them, for servants, of the posterity of Ham; and that as the Gospel prevails, this blessing shall be enjoyed more and more in all the families of Shem and Japheth.

Do any of us realize the trouble and suffering, expense and loss, borne in a multitude of families at the North and East, because we either have no servants, or capricious and unfaithful ones? It seems hard to find or keep those who are willing to do what is required. One great desire is, for servants that are servants, such as our Saviour mentioned—Luke xvii. 8, 9—that do not require waiting upon. The evil has grown so great, that it is now the great drawback to the happiness and comfort of our families. The evil bears hard on our wives and daughters; it is an affliction that is fast wearing them out, and carrying many of them to the grave before their time. It probably prevents the union and formation of many families. We forget that God nowhere in His Word declares that the German and Irish shall serve others, therefore we ought not to expect too much from them. As descendants of Japheth, they are also entitled to the service of the children of Ham, and will, doubtless, as circumstances admit, be served by them.

So far as we know, there was no provision made for servants in the family before the flood. From the record made of Lamech, he must for awhile have toiled along alone: "And Lamech lived a hundred eighty and two years, and begat a son, and called his name Noah, saying, This same shall comfort us concerning our work and toil of our hands, because of the ground which the Lord hath cursed."

As we read God's Word and providence, He took advantage of the sin and defection of Ham to devote his posterity to be servants in the families of Shem and Japheth, whom He blessed; and that this provision made for their families shall last as long as time, and be enjoyed more in the ages to come than it has been in the generations past. That it is, in fact, "the heritage of the heathen," a blessing of the Gospel He has promised "to give His people." That it is our duty and privilege to accept of this great gift from the hand of God, and that we ought not to undervalue or despise it; if we do, we must expect more loss and trouble in household affairs.

Would it not tend to advance the welfare of all our families, if we had one or more faithful Africans to aid us in the drudgery of life? While receiving from them bodily help, we, like guardians, could care for and impart truths that would make them wise and happy for time and eternity.

You may search the world over in vain to find more faithful or affectionate servants than the Africans. The relation of master and servant being for life, and in its true and best estate satisfactory to both, there grows up an attachment for each other. The servant loves his master and family, and is faithful to their interests, proved in ten thousand instances in the every-day life of the institution.

What better inheritance can a man pass down to his children to bridge over the gap, than faithful, well-trained servants? such as Abraham of old turned over to his son Isaac, to help and counsel him in his younger days; and what better position can the poor African have, than a place in some God-fearing and obeying family? We say God-fearing and obeying, for we hold to the doctrine that this institution will be perfected more and more as the *Gospel prevails.*

Ye descendants of Shem and Japheth, see what provisions God has made for your help in this institution of bond-servants, for which the world will yet praise and thank Him! And you, who are of the posterity of Ham, behold the goodness of your God! In His wrath He hath remembered mercy; He has tempered His justice with His love in so ordering it in His providence, as He seems to have done, that you shall not abide alone on this earth, out off from fellowship with the rest of the world; but has planted you in the families of the righteous, so that your vine may run up their olive tree, that while you protect their trunk from the heat of the day, and they eat of the fruit of your labor, they cover your defenseless head while you partake of the oil and fatness that drop from the branches. What harmony! There is no conflict, but beautiful harmony, in all the works of God.

The Psalmist says, Ethiopia* shall soon stretch out her hands unto God. The sons of Africa stretch out the hands of their strength to work for the bread that sustains our bodies. if we will but feed their famished souls with the bread of life.

A day of better things must soon dawn on the children of Africa; for when the nations shall know by the Word of God their right in them, He will dispose the nations, by the influence of His spirit, to treat the sons or daughters of Africa according to the precepts of His Word.

If the New Englanders will search some of their old church records, they will find sufficient evidence that many of their fathers who held slaves, did, in imitation of the Patriarch Abraham, and in obedience to the covenant God commanded him—Gen. xvii. 12, 13 : " He that is born in the house, or bought with money of any stranger, which is not of thy seed. He that is born in thy house, and he that is bought with thy money, must needs be circumcised : and my covenant shall be in your flesh for an everlasting covenant ;" which ceremony was changed to baptism, by the command of our Saviour, as held by many. Many of their fathers as they will find, brought the children of their slaves into the church, and had them baptized, agreeing themselves to teach them the truths of the Gospel as they grew up.

There used to be this proverb current among some of the negroes in New England—how extensively in use we can not say—" 'Tis as scarce as the Catechism." The meaning of which was, that when slavery was abolished in those States, the late masters felt they were free from responsibility, therefore did not care for the body or soul of their late bond-servants, as formerly, and so neglected to teach them the Catechism, which they loved to have taught them; so when anything was scarce, in comparison the negro would say, "It was scarce as the Catechism."

* Ethiopia, in Hebrew, is—" Cush"—" Blackness, or I burn."

In the matter of the treaty made by Joshua with the Gibeonites —part of the tribe of the Hivites, descendants of Canaan, of the posterity of Ham—as recorded in Joshua ix., the opinion prevails generally that Joshua and the elders did wrong to make the treaty, and that if they had asked counsel of the Lord, He would not have allowed them to make it, but would have rejected the suit of the Gibeonites. Joshua and the elders were wrong, certainly, in not consulting with the Lord, as directed in His Word.

We have an opinion, supported by several reasons, that God, who knows the end from the beginning, and neither does nor allows anything to be done without some wise purpose, would, if He had been consulted, have consented to the treaty, at the same time removing the vail of deception. The first reason is, that the Gibeonites must have given up their idolatry and acknowledged the true God, as it appears, from the context and their confession, they did; and not only that, but offered themselves to God and the Israelites as bond-servants.

"God's promises and threatenings are always to be restrained and limited under the conditions of obedience and repentance, though these conditions be often concealed," as appears by Jer. xviii. 7, 8: "At what instant I shall speak concerning a nation, and concerning a kingdom, to pluck up, and pull down, and destroy; if that nation, against whom I have pronounced, turn from their evil, I will repent of the evil that I thought to do unto them." This was verified in the mission of Jonah to Nineveh, and we think in this case of the Gibeonites also.

One of the reasons are the many instructive lessons to be drawn from the entire history, as recorded in the Bible, of the Gibeonites, afterward called "Nethinims," the meaning of which was "offered."

Another, and a leading reason with us is, that the transactions and interesting history of this people are but a type or shadow of what shall take place when the Jews shall go back to Jerusalem and to their own land, as we believe the Word of God declares they will. The prophet Zechariah says, that when they shall go back, "That ten men shall take hold out of all languages of the nations, even shall take hold of the skirt of him that is a Jew, saying, We will go with you: for we have heard that God is with you." The sons of Africa must be of the "ten." *Isaac's* blessing to Jacob was, "Let people serve thee." The prophet Isaiah says, "That when the waste cities shall be built, then strangers shall stand and feed your flocks, and the sons of the alien shall be your plowmen and your vine-dressers."

One of the most important texts to prove that the Gibeonites, in offering themselves to Joshua and to the Israelites, as bond-servants forever, are but a type of what shall yet be done when the Jews again enter Canaan, is to be found in Isaiah xlv. 14: "Thus saith the Lord, The labor of Egypt, and merchandise of Ethiopia and of the Sabeans, men of stature, shall come over *unto thee, and they shall be thine :* they shall come after thee; in chains they shall come over, and they shall fall down unto thee, they shall make supplication unto thee, saying, Surely God is in thee; and there is none else, there is no God. Verily thou art a God that hidest thyself, O God of Israel, the Saviour."

The laborers of Egypt, Ethiopia, and the Sabeans—men of stature—shall come over to *thee,* and shall be thine in chains; they shall come, that is as bond-servants, glad to be their bond-servants, because God is with them.* If this view be right, it is only another incidental proof that this system of bond-servants shall be in full existence when the Church is in its best estate. When the Jews return to Canaan, a vast deal of work will have to be done to build again the waste places, and they will have great need of men of stature and strength. Fletcher, in his work on Brazil, states, that on the coffee plantations there is a race of Afri-

* The following extract is from an old copy, published in London, some two hundred years since, of "Annotations of the Bible," written by a number of learned divines, some of whom had been engaged in the celebrated translation, called "King James' version :" Joshua ix. 23 ("Now therefore ye are cursed.") "Because ye have not endeavored to preserve your lives by lawful means, but by lying and dissembling, therefore in respect to your temporal condition, you have brought upon yourselves and your children this heavy curse of bondage and servitude. In denouncing of which he may seem to relate unto that prophetical curse pronounced by Noah against Cham, their great progenitor, that he should be a servant of servants unto his brethren, the which was now verified in his posterity.—Gen. ix. 25. But yet this curse, through God's infinite mercy, became in some respects a blessing to these Gibeonites, seeing by these services (though base in themselves) they had near approach unto God, in the service of the sanctuary, for the good of their souls, and were in sort given and consecrated unto God, as the name afterward given them doth import; for these were, as is thought, those Nethinims, of whom we read—1 Chron. ix. 2; Ezra ii. 43—whose office was to attend upon the Levites in the service of the sanctuary, who, though from the first beginning they were employed in this service, yet are said to be appointed by David and the princes unto it in respect that they did order and dispose of them in their several turns and courses.—Ezra viii. 20. Now, if David himself, 'though a great king, chose rather to be a doorkeeper in the house of his God than to dwell in the tents of wickedness'—Ps. lxxxiv. 10 —then these poor Gibeonites had no damage by their base services, seeing by them they had this privilege of near approaches unto God." [The above remarkable annotation coincides with our views, which we have discovered since writing the preceding pages.]

cans of larger stature and more strength than what we have at the South.

King David speaks of the Israelites inheriting the labor of the heathen.

These Gibeonites—these bond-servants—were always faithful (as far as we can learn) to the Israelites—for more than a thousand years never engaging against them in the wars in which Judah and Israel were involved, going and returning with them into and from captivity.

When Ezra returned from the captivity, it seems that many more Nethinims or Gibeonites returned with him than he could persuade of the Levites to return. According to Nehemiah, they helped to repair the walls of Jerusalem. Take them altogether, they are a modest example of faithfulness, that the world has not observed and can not appreciate.

It seems, as a class, they were kept separate, in their true place, doing the work originally assigned them, and that they did not intermingle or intermarry with any other race.

According to Ezra (probably by his advice, as he undoubtedly regarded them with favor), the King Artaxerxes decreed that no poll-tax, tribute, or custom should be imposed upon them.

Here at the North we have practically expelled the African from all our churches, and will not allow him to have fellowship or worship with us. We have sinned greatly in this matter. If we have good preaching of the Gospel, they have a right to enjoy it with us, for its privileges and blessings were purchased for all.

We should, for many reasons, adopt the practice of the South, and let the Africans occupy our galleries, and join with us in hymns of praise. At the South we have seen a host of them, in the well-filled galleries, rise and join in the song, the full chorus of which, we thought, was sweeter and more impressive than anything we had elsewhere heard.

It is worthy of remark how willingly, if not gladly, the Gibeonites offered themselves and accepted the condition of bond-servants; as with a sort of instinctive sense that it was their true place and best condition—where a blessing was to be found.

Years ago, fresh from the North, and on Southern ground, we viewed the system, and saw around us the subjects of it largely in the majority. We wondered at first why there appeared to be no discontent; we could discover no thought of trying to free themselves from their condition. We knew that if the matter was reversed, and we were one to one hundred Africans, we should not cease thought nor effort till we had got clear from the condition.

There was no other conclusion for us to arrive at, than that God had given them what He had not us, a nature and disposition for the condition, and a sort of instinctive sense that in no other place would their happiness be so much promoted. From that time we have had no particular fear of trouble or insurrection among the Africans in our land. Bad blood, evil counsels, neglect of teaching and training, may sometimes cause some local difficulty; but farther than that, we have never given any credence to insurrection stories in a Gospel land like ours. St. Domingo will be cited by some, but in that island there were nearly ten blacks to one white—many of the blacks fresh from Africa and uncivilized—scarcely any on the island taught the truths of the Gospel; nearly all driven to the extreme, and excited also by Jacobin and turbulent spirits from France, we could expect nothing less.

It is well for us to have even more confidence than we have had in our servants. What fault have we in our land to find after two hundred years' service from them?

Look again at the same race—the Gibeonites. More than four hundred years after they offered themselves to Joshua and became bond-servants, God punished the Israelites, for breaking their part of the treaty, with a famine of three years. But not a word was offered in excuse that the Gibeonites had not been faithful in every respect to their part of the agreement; if they had broken any part of the treaty, it would, no doubt, have been mentioned. This is wonderful, when we consider how many times the children of Israel had been in bondage. It would seem as if the Almighty guaranteed their faithfulness. So let us have no particular fears about our bond-servants, but give them all liberty consistent with order, morals, and a faithful performance of duty. When ministers of the Gospel explain all these things to them, you may expect a still greater degree of contentment.

We know that there are some that look into the newspapers daily, expecting to hear that the negroes have risen and massacred their masters, perhaps with a sort of curiosity, like the man who followed the menagerie, expecting to see the lion kill the keeper as he entered the cage. If any expect to see such a general insurrection in our land, they may look into the papers till they are as old as Methuselah, and die without the sight. The one enters the cage of the lion against nature—the other holds the bond-servant in the providence of God.

Many who will not lift their finger to alleviate the wants of the poor negro at their doors, are in distress about the far-off slave, and even feel offended because he will make no effort to secure his freedom—a feeling somewhat akin to that of the hen who raised the brood of ducks, and when for the first time she saw them take to the water, in great distress called them back, and when they would not obey, retired in disgust, because they would not leave what to her seemed a miserable condition. She, like others, could not understand that that was their second or instinctive nature.

A few, a very few we hope, like Job's wife, tell the poor Africans at the South: "Curse God and die;" "Kill your master and be free." And the poor African, like Job, replies : "Thou speakest as one of the foolish women speakest." "What! shall we receive good at the hand of God, and shall we not receive evil?" Like Job, they will have their reward.

It is of vital importance that the institution of bond-servants should have only such form and character as God has marked out in His Word, and such as His providence and the experience of good men teach. From Leviticus xxv. 45, 46, we may learn some lessons of great value to direct us in this matter.

One of the first is, that good men are best entitled to hold bond-servants, for the obvious reason that the servant will be better off in every respect with an upright and good man, or in his family, than one that is the reverse. Notice the command was issued to the Israelites to buy bond-servants. The Israelites here, as a nation, represent all true Gospel nations. The next question, Of whom shall we buy bond-servants? The answer, Of the heathen; the reason is plain.

For what purpose shall we buy them? The candid mind will be satisfied that the true answer is, The necessary use we have for the service that has to be performed, and which we require of them; not for speculation, not to be made merchandise of, to be sold and resold for gain; but those who need them shall buy them. The marginal reading of King James' translation has the Hebrew: "Shall serve yourselves of them forever." Some older translations have it: "Shall use their labor forever." How long shall we keep them? "Forever." When we die we must pass them to our children for a possession, for that appears to be the command. To set them free does not appear to be authorized. We must care for them when they are young, in middle life, in old age; we must care for them to the end.

As a rule, it is really better for the servant to have one master for life than many. Their attachments are not broken off; but both it and the instructions given to him and his children, all have a chance to ripen into fruit. You well know how the faithful bond-servants, old men and women that have been long in your families;

and brought up with you, are loved and honored ; you will not suffer them to be harmed.

The faithful bond-servant cares for his master's interest, and loves his children oftentimes more than he loves his own. There is a marked difference in these respects between him and the hireling, who cares but little for the sheep or the pasture.

The light-hearted African, sociable and affectionate in his nature, loves his master's home, and if faithful, ought not, if possible, to be sent far away from it. If it is necessary that the master or his family should part with him, some purchaser should be found near home, on the principle laid down in the law of Moses, that the next of kin should redeem the Hebrew or his possession. The old Patriarchs, as they moved, took their servants with them. But what seems singular is, that when the Jews went into Babylonian captivity, they carried their servants, the posterity of Ham, with them, and brought them back when they returned ; or what appears to be the truth, those bond-servants voluntarily returned.

In regard to marriage, we do not learn that a bond-servant has any better right to marry without his master's consent than the child has without the father's, and the one in this matter ought not to be unreasonable any more than the other. Circumstances control the event. When married, the relation ought to be regarded, and it might be well to have a family record kept, of which the master might take charge. In time it would be of value, and become a matter of pride to the servant. So far from interfering with his service or the value of his labor, it would tend to make him more valuable. It will be seen, from the records of Ezra and Nehemiah, that the Gibeonites imitated the Israelites in this matter, kept a record, and were able to trace the line back hundreds of years. They prided themselves on keeping the stock pure, and separated themselves from the mixed seed. The institution will not bear the cross in the blood; it breeds trouble; the Word of God is against it. The rule for the mixed seed, in the end, may have to be freedom, and not servitude ; they may have to dwell outside, and not in the family. The true master will not spoil his servant by being too indulgent, nor make him unhappy by being too exacting ; and as for correction (for there are times when it is necessary), he will know what is most suitable and sufficient; for some, one form is better than another. St. Paul says : He that will not work shall not eat. An intelligent and Christian lady from Alabama informed us the past season, that she could bring her servants to terms and to duty quicker by depriving them of a meal than by any other method.

At the South, all know how readily the servant is to honor his master and pay respect to the white man ; so, for their sakes, let us not bring any unnecessary reproach on them. Let us call them, in conversation and in documents, servants (which they are), and not slaves. One great reason why we should leave off the name of *slaves* or *slavery* is, because of the false meaning or idea attached to it by many at the North, viz., that those who are under its condition are subject to the vile or slavish passions of men. If it were not unchristian, we might retort and say, " they judge others by themselves."

The Christian father may give his son a lesson of filial obedience and make him know the need of Christ, when he points him to the mark of disobedience that Ham got for his children when he dishonored his father, and that a like mark of an evil heart all of us inherit from our father Adam, and that, finally, all marks or appearance of sin are to be washed away from those who receive the atoning blood of the Son of God.

It ought not to be forgotten that when the Gibeonites offered themselves as bond-servants to Joshua, that he first supplied the Levites—the ministers and priests of God—with servants to assist them in all the more laborious parts of God's worship. (The work given them to do, if it was laborious, was also simple, for which they were probably best adapted.) King David afterward took good care to provide the Levites with a full supply of these bond-servants, as it is recorded by those men of good common sense and practical judgment, as well as piety, Ezra and Nehemiah. Now from this we learn, that those who preach the Gospel among us ought not to be forgotten. Many are the offices and duties they are called upon to perform for the congregations of which they have charge ; and which are often neglected, because the hands of the pastor and his wife are tied at home. The congregation that will give one or two bond-servants to the pastor will be multiplying his hands and increasing his ability to work for the spiritual good of his people. As for the servant, he would esteem it a place of privilege and blessing. Those who break unto us the bread of eternal life, and invite us unto the fountains of living waters, should be freely supplied with the bread and water of this life, that they daily stand in need of.

To what practical use shall we put the doctrines inculcated in these pages ?

It is the first duty of those who have faith in the institution of bond-servants to set forth the ground upon which it is established, to make known all its advantages, and defend it from all attacks.

Political parties are not so much its friends or enemies as public opinion, on which many think the whole system rests, and with it must rise or fall. But we do not so think. One word from God is worth more to us than the voice of the world against it. Public opinion now at the North is against the institution; and why? Because its enemies have given it a character that suited them, then tried it by that character before the public, and a partial verdict has of course been rendered. Its friends, having undoubted confidence in it, have neglected its defense—have not presented the evidence at hand in its favor; and some would, now that the decision is against it, declare that the court had no jurisdiction over them, and they were not bound by it, or that they would separate themselves from its power and influence. The true plan is, to have the verdict set aside, rendered on the partial testimony of men who have the appearance of truth, love, and equity, but really destitute of all; demand a new trial, and not go out of the court of public opinion till its advocates have given it the high character it deserves. Employ able advocates, who shall make it their business to defend it as it ought to be, meeting the many high-wrought, fictitious stories with the truth; the false statements, by the thousand facts in its favor; the insinuations and false charges, by honest intentions and acts, not allowing its good to be evil spoken of. Let its advocates uncover the foundation, and show the court the rock upon which it is built; let them turn and exhibit the original charter, and the many years it has been in possession, and there need be no fear of the result.

. We have never yet heard of any society formed at the South to defend and advocate the institution, while there have been many at the North formed to destroy it. Is it any wonder that they have undermined its influence?

They have caused to be written across the institution, in black letters, the word "sin." If in view of its progenitor, its human cause, Ham, it is written sin, let it be so. If in view of the unbelief in which it is held, and the unfair means taken to drive it out of the world, it is written sin, let it be so. It is the duty of those who have faith in it, to turn on the other side and write, in golden letters, "righteous!" because of the righteous judgment of God on the posterity of Ham. Because the true effect of the system in this life is to make the subjects of it "righteous." Because, by obedience to its condition, many are led to the Saviour, who is "righteous."

The South is so identified with the system, that its character and reputation stands or falls with it; and therefore it is important that she should come to its defense, and be justified for holding it. *Independence* is not what she wants, but *justification* throughout the Union and the world. She is really as independent in the Union as she could be out of it, and we sincerely trust she will give up all idea of going out, as being unnecessary for the vindication of her honor, rights, and equality. A true and better way opens before her, where all may be secured, and her welfare greatly promoted.

The right to separate from the rest of the Union we do not discuss. The abstract right to separate, to our minds, is clear, when the Constitution, or compact of agreement, is pers' tently broken in letter and spirit. But the right is not so clear, in good faith, to separate from those who have resisted, with all their might and influence, all infractions of the Constitution. Something is due to them, and that, too, in proportion to their honest efforts, their numbers, their character, and influence.

If the South act somewhat on the same principle that governed the Almighty, when He said He would spare the cities of the plain if there were found fifty righteous men in them, they would not, at this time, cut loose from the North, thereby involving in one common ruin friend and foe, at the North and South.

If the men of the South would look at this matter in its true light; take a view of the band of men that have stood up nobly for their rights and our rights, without hope of reward or interest in the matter, only so far as they loved to have constitutional principles prevail and the country prosper—we say if the South could take a look, *and become acquainted* with these men, she would never think of parting company with them. She would feel assured that she might count upon them, in the hour of danger, to defend her rights when they were assailed. Holding fast to such a stronghold, she would know certainly, that in the end, her cause must triumph. These motives are sufficient for the South to hold fast to her friends, and the Union and Constitution as it is, without mentioning the convulsions, the losses, and the distresses that must follow at the South and at the North the disruption of this Union, that God has made, cemented as it has been by the blood of the best of men. No! we do not believe this Union is to be broken up. We have strong faith in it, and the institution in it that seems to be in jeopardy. We believe that God has great purposes yet to perform with both. We believe that a greater measure of prosperity is immediately before and for this Union than it has ever yet seen; that so far from losing or parting with any of its members, it will gain in numbers and in territory; that soon there will be more unity, oneness in interest, feeling, and sentiment North and South, East and West, than we have had for a generation; that we shall yet welcome at the North, in the summer of joy, our Southern friends with their servants, and we, in the winter of life, with our servants, partake, in the sunny South, of their hospitality; that railing and discord will give place to peace and harmony, and that good feeling and kind words shall everywhere abound.

The interest, prosperity, and happiness of the people in this Union are one and inseparable. We must thrive or suffer together. One section can not suffer without all more or less participating. This is the natural law and course of things. One section is not to be built up at the expense of another. Sometimes they are by unequal legislation. But we can not learn that it is any part of the plan of the Almighty that one section or country should thrive at the cost of another, when everything is left to take its natural course. Our prosperity and happiness are mutual, and ought so to be considered by every one.

In this country, among the people at large, there is really no conflict or war of interest; but there is truly a conflict of ideas between the North and South. A party in the North, and a party in England, hold ideas that influence their action every way it can be brought to bear against an interest—an institution vital to the South and important to the world. This abolition—this emancipation idea—this idea that bond-service *per se* is a sin—is an enemy, and must be put down, because it is not supported by truth, and produces evil. With that idea we must war till the truth prevails in our land not only, but in the world. The ideas for and against the institution are antagonistic, and one or the other must give way before we can have peace and prosperity, whether the Union be destroyed or not. " Can two walk together except they are agreed ?"

As we believe the institution finds support in the truth and providence of God, and in its true state and place is good for all concerned, so we think it ought to be defended, perfected, and extended, where all who wish to reap the fruits of it may enjoy it.

Peace, and not discord, is the rule when everything is in and kept in its true place. The idea that there is an irrepressible conflict between free labor and bond labor, between the free-servant and the bond-servant, so that one or the other must perish, is false in theory and fact. The idea brought forward at this time is only a new application of the old and envious notion of the Evil-One (the great disturber), that one man's welfare and happiness stands in the way of another, and therefore he must be got out of the way. They can with just as much truth say that there is an irrepressible conflict between the labor of the man and of the woman.

In fact, the free labor and laborer of the North, and of the world, has been greatly benefited by the bond labor of the South. Even the fear now prevailing that the free labor of the North will be separated from the bond labor of the South, is operating to throw tens and hundreds of thousands of honest, dependent laborers out of employment.

As a people, we trust we shall soon walk together as one man, for the common sense of the people must perceive that where every one is working in his true place, the welfare of all must be promoted.

This great question that so concerns our faith and practice, our peace and prosperi*,, has, in its present attitude and relations, engaged our earnest consideration for more than a year past. In its investigation we have been animated with a single desire to arrive at the whole truth concerning it, in order that we might know what was right and ought to be done, and in what way the country might escape the evils of commotion and civil war, and every man be at peace with his neighbor, esteeming his brother man, no matter from what section he came, as good or better than himself.

In the preceding pages we have stated what are our honest convictions of the truth ; and now, if we might be allowed to suggest, would state what we think are the first steps to be taken to *prevent dissolution, and bring about, eventually, harmonious action,* which are : *That the people in the States where the institution exists, shall unite in choosing from their intelligent, upright men, of practical experience and judgment, delegates to meet in Convention early in the coming year, that they may decide upon such simple and uniform laws and regulations as they shall deem best and necessary, to recommend to the Legislature of the several States, in order to perfect the institution for the good of masters and servants, as far as it is in their power to do it. Also, to publish facts concerning the system, for the information and benefit of the people; and on the assembling of the coming Congress, knock at the doors of our National Legislative halls for the repeal of the laws in the way of the importation of bond-servants from Africa, and for the passage of proper laws to protect the same. It would be well, also, to organize a society for the protection of African bond-servants and for the defense of the institution.*

If the South would but turn its energies in the direction named, they could do it with good hope of success ; for we think, on a full consideration of the whole matter, this course would meet the approval of tens and hundreds of thousands at the North, and would give to all, whether they approved or not, immediate and undoubted confidence in the permanence of the Union and stability of the General Government, and high prosperity of all the people in all their various interests.

We would at least have before us the prospect that we should once more be in feeling and sentiment a united people, as we were in the Revolution, in the days of our fathers, when Christian men had more influence and control in national affairs.

To lay aside for a moment the mere question of right or wrong, it would be altogether a better policy for the South to step from behind her ramparts of defense, advance Scipio-like, and carry the war into Africa, contest the battle on that ground, where victory would be sure to follow. In so doing there would be nothing risked, and everything might be gained. The minds and bodies of men both tire in occupying and defending for a long time the same ground, especially when satisfied they ought to possess more.

We have, in view of the light of God's Word, His providential acts, and the experience and history of the races, stated in these pages what are our honest convictions of the truth concerning the institution of "African servitude," and the course it is best now to pursue in reference to it, which we have felt it to be our duty thus to publish. And now we have only to say, that as a Christian nation, we ought with cheerful hope and grateful confidence to turn our national troubles over to God our Father, being assured that He cares for us, and will yet make the truth and right appear.

> " His love in time past
> Forbids us to think
> He'll leave us at last
> In trouble to sink."